The Baby Laundry for Unmarried Mothers

The Baby Laundry for Unmarried Mothers

Angela Patrick

With Lynne Barrett-Lee

**SIMON &
SCHUSTER**

London · New York · Sydney · Toronto · New Delhi

A CBS COMPANY

First published in Great Britain by Simon & Schuster UK Ltd, 2012
A CBS COMPANY

5 7 9 10 8 6

Simon & Schuster UK Ltd
1st Floor
222 Gray's Inn Road
London WC1X 8HB

www.simonandschuster.co.uk

Simon & Schuster Australia, Sydney
Simon & Schuster India, New Delhi

A CIP catalogue record for this book
is available from the British Library.

ISBN 978-1-84983-490-2

Typeset in Fournier by M Rules
Printed and bound by CPI Group (UK) Ltd, Croydon, CR0 4YY

While this book endeavours to give a faithful account of the author's experiences,
some names, places and dates have been changed to protect the privacy of
the individuals involved and in order to best represent the story.

For my son

Contents

PART THREE

PART ONE

Chapter One

The Swinging Sixties. It's funny people still call them that and like to hang on to the rose-tinted notion that it was the decade to end all decades — the 'sex, drugs and rock 'n' roll' one. It was the decade of which it was famously said that if you could remember anything about it, you weren't really there. But for me, and many like me, that notion didn't hold true: I was there, and I remember it all too well.

February 1963

His name was Peter and for a time I was captivated by him.

He wasn't especially tall – around five foot ten, no more than that; not much taller than me, in fact, and I liked to wear high heels – but he was solidly built, powerful. He looked like he could take care of himself. And I could imagine him taking care of me, too.

'Susan Maughan,' he was saying to me now. '*That's* who I've just realised you remind me of – Susan Maughan.'

I was bending down, trying to wriggle my feet out of my

black patent high heels, while he held my drink for me. 'Who?' I said, rising.

'Susan Maughan,' he said again. 'And do you ever last a whole evening without taking off your shoes?'

I considered his question: not very often was the answer. I liked the extra height but I also liked dancing, and you couldn't dance in winkle-pickers with high stiletto heels – not without suffering the consequences. I knew that well, because the night I'd met Peter at the Ilford Palais, a favourite haunt of mine, I'd danced the night away and definitely suffered the next morning.

We were having a terrible, bitter winter in both temperature and duration – it was already being flagged up as the worst since just after the war. The trudge back home through the snow from Rayleigh station in Essex hadn't helped my aching feet. Numb with cold in my just-to-the-knee skirt, my legs and feet blue and mottled, I hadn't realised just how bad my blisters were. I hobbled around painfully for days afterwards.

It was still freezing a fortnight later. Though much of the snow had gone, there were still dirty piles of it on the pavements. With ice now lying in treacherous sheets everywhere the snow had been, going out for the evening was something of an endurance test – not that I cared. I was nineteen and having the best time imaginable: I had my job in the City, I'd got a great bunch of friends and now I had a new boyfriend too.

'I'm taking them off so we can dance, silly,' I told him, as he passed me back my drink. I took a sip from it and grimaced. It tasted horrible. It was a snowball, haphazardly mixed, and much too strong for me. I couldn't drink it, but I didn't need it and wouldn't finish it, I decided. I put it down again, with exaggerated care, on a low corner table. I had to nudge an overflowing glass ashtray out of the way to make room for it.

'Susan Maughan?' I said incredulously. 'I don't look anything like Susan Maughan!' Susan Maughan sang 'Bobby's Girl', and seemed to be everywhere. She wore her eyeliner a bit like I did, but that, to my mind, was where our similarities ended.

Someone had put 'Losing You', by Brenda Lee, on the record player. 'Anyway,' I said, looking up at him, if only slightly. 'Are we dancing or aren't we?'

He slipped an arm around my waist and kicked my shoes under the table for me. 'Oh, yes,' he said, reeling me in to him. 'We are.'

The party was at the house of a friend of a friend of Peter's. I didn't know which friend or which friend of that friend it was, but it was in Loughton, in Essex, in an unremarkable suburban semi. As was almost invariably the case with house parties, the parents of the friend of the friend were away. Almost all of us would be staying until the morning. Few boys had cars back then, girls almost never drove, and there was practically nothing in the way of public transport late at night. So I'd be staying over, even though officially (as far as my mother was concerned, anyway) I was staying at my friend Sandra's.

It had been a busy night. After work, we'd gone to another favourite haunt, a new mocha bar in Leicester Square, which Sandra and I loved. It was run by a family of ebullient Italians, who made amazing cakes and gateaux to go with their frothy coffee. They had a jukebox, too, which made the place something of a draw. We'd stayed for an hour, waiting for Peter and his mates to arrive, chatting and listening to the music: Cliff Richard and the Shadows, the Beach Boys, Frank Ifield, as well as a brilliant new band everyone was talking about called The Beatles, who'd just brought out their first record. And then Peter had arrived and told us about the house party. You never turned down a chance to go to a house party.

It had been a good one, too, so far. It was around eleven by now and we were both a bit tipsy. Though I was swaying along with the music, I might have been swaying anyway. I'd barely eaten since the cake earlier, my stomach too full of impossible-to-quell butterflies to make room for the Scotch eggs and sandwiches and bowls of peanuts that someone had laid out in the kitchen.

I'd been seeing Peter for just over a fortnight. We'd met several times before, but now we were officially a couple, and I was still slightly reeling from the knowledge that someone I liked so much seemed keen on me too. I'd been in love just once, the previous year, and the boy had been the one to end it. I'd been inconsolable, so broken-hearted that I thought I'd never get over it. I'd felt unlovable for so long.

But no more, it seemed. Peter and I had been for a drink and to the pictures – to see the recently released and brilliant *Summer Holiday*, starring Cliff Richard – and, last weekend, had gone back together to the Ilford Palais, where hanging off the arm of such a good-looking guy had been the most thrilling thing I'd felt in a long time.

My late father, who was ex-army and a real stickler for detail, would have approved of Peter. He was so smart, such a stylish dresser, and always beautifully turned out. It may be superficial, but one thing I seemed to have inherited from my father was a sense that such details *did* matter in a man. 'You can tell a lot about the inside,' he would say, 'from what's outside.' I knew Peter would definitely have passed muster.

Even without my father there to approve of him, I really liked him, and felt a delicious shiver run through me every time our eyes met. We'd come to the party as a group, but now the group had disappeared, and what might happen next, I didn't know.

'It's your hair,' he whispered as we made repeated slow rotations in time to the music, the view of the wallpaper, violently hued and patterned (presumably to compete with the carpet), forcing me to close my eyes to escape the glare.

'What about it?' I said, opening them again, dimly aware that except for one other smooching couple and Brenda Lee we were alone.

'You wear yours just like she does. You know – all big and flicky.'

'Not intentionally,' I answered. Even though I sort of did sometimes, but not quite: mine was longer and that detail seemed to matter. How had he not noticed?

He must have sensed that there was something a bit indignant in the way I said this, because he pulled back then and pretended to frown. His eyes were dark and mesmerising. They were the most attractive thing about him – that and his Mediterranean good looks and his smile. 'Sorry,' he said, turning the frown into a smile for me now. 'I'll rephrase that: I meant that she tries to wear hers a bit like *yours*. Though she's *obviously* not as pretty . . .'

He came close again, grinning boyishly at his unsubtle attempt at flattery. Then he kissed me, and kept kissing me till the record ended. No one came and replaced it with Susan Maughan or anyone else. It just crackled on, round and round the turntable, the stylus quietly talking to itself. More time passed. More revolutions of the little living room. More kissing. Then his mouth was at my ear again. 'Shall we go upstairs?'

I wasn't drunk. I wasn't gripped by a fierce, irresistible longing, but I did feel attracted to him. I was sweet on him. I enjoyed being his girlfriend. I adored that he seemed to be so taken with me. He was a 'catch', to use the parlance: desirable, charming. He was *extremely* charming, and I knew I was being charmed by him tonight. As a consequence, I was a little out of my depth, and aware of it – though not in a frightened way – but it didn't seem to matter. The voice telling me to keep my head was present, but I was comfortable ignoring it – for the moment, at least. It wasn't as if I was going to go all the way with him, however hard he might try to charm me, was it? Even though it seemed everyone else did it these days.

Glancing around the living room, its gloomy lighting making a blur of all the hard edges of my thinking, I realised the other couple, whom I didn't know, had disappeared. There was a low throb of voices coming from the kitchen, but they were male. I also realised I hadn't seen Sandra in a while, but that didn't surprise me: I vaguely remembered she'd seemed to be getting on well with a boy she'd confessed to having her eye on for some time.

It was as if the party had ground to a halt without us noticing. Or, rather, it had imperceptibly become another sort of party – one in which everyone seemed to have something other than dancing on their minds.

'Hmm?' said Peter, nuzzling my neck. 'C'mon. Let's go up, yeah?'

I left my shoes where they were and let him lead me up the stairs.

Chapter Two

September 1963

'This is your stop, love,' the woman sitting on the bench seat beside me whispered. 'And that's the place,' she added, pointing. 'See it? That's the convent, that is. That big place over there.'

It was mid-afternoon on a warm autumnal weekday, and I was struggling with two things as I alighted from the bus: the first was my battered suitcase, which resisted me as I struggled to wrench it from under the stairwell, and the second was the knowledge that my travelling companion was able not only to point out which bus stop I needed, but also knew where I was going and why. I was seven months pregnant.

I was probably pink from the shame – how had she *known* that was where I was going? – but also hot, much too hot, in my heavy duster coat. It was burnt orange in colour and the height of current fashion, as it was in a style Doris Day often wore in her films. It had a boat neck and was fastened by two oversized buttons; A-line in shape, it flared to the knee. But for all its fashionable styling, it was a cruel irony that it had been bought for one purpose: to hide the evidence of my terrible secret.

My new temporary home rose to greet me as I walked wearily from the bus stop, my great size, coupled with the heat, sapping what little energy I had. I'd been given directions and the address of my destination, and the paper on which I'd scribbled them was crumpled in my free hand. I felt a crumb of comfort on arriving at last. At least here, or so I thought, I would be free of the subterfuge of the past few months. At least here I would no longer have to hide or lie. At least here I would no longer have to force my body into a tight rubber corset so the growing bulge of my baby didn't give me away.

But as I dragged my case awkwardly up the furrows of the thickly gravelled drive, those feelings were soon replaced with a sense of anxiety and foreboding. With its ugly buildings, precisely manicured lawns and towering conifers, the Loreto Convent Mother and Baby Home for Unmarried Mothers didn't look like a place in which comfort would be found. In fact, it looked every bit as grim and forbidding as its name; its imposing brick façade and Victorian sash windows suggesting that nothing but unhappiness lay within.

My ears were already straining for sounds of life beyond the heavy front door, for routine everyday sounds that might set my fears to rest, but the silence was complete. I felt light headed and frightened. I wanted nothing more passionately than to run away, but there was nowhere to run. I could see a distortion of my own anguished face in the shiny brass knocker. As I stood there, the only sound that of incongruous birdsong, I knew exactly what sort of welcome to expect. I had brought shame on myself, on my family and on the Catholic Church; the nuns who were to care for me therefore had another, more important job: to see to it that I atoned for my sins.

Ignoring the knocker in favour of the brass bell set into the doorframe, I pushed the button with my finger and waited, my heart in my mouth. It seemed a long time before I could hear the muffled sound of approaching footsteps, followed by a latch being turned. The door opened to reveal a large entrance hall with a polished wooden floor, in the middle of which rose a staircase. Beyond that, the increasingly dim vista revealed several panelled doors, which presumably led to other parts of the house.

Directly before me stood a nun: she was tall, though slightly stooped, and dressed in a full-length black habit. A perfect oval of wizened face, shielded by metal-rimmed glasses, sat encircled by a pristine white wimple. There was no smile of greeting, no gesture of welcome, just a scowl of displeasure and irritation.

'Yes?' she said. She looked as if she'd lived for about seventy years, and had the demeanour of someone who'd found little to smile about during any of them. There was nothing remotely grandmotherly about her.

I slipped my piece of paper, now damp and limp, back into my coat pocket. 'I'm Angela Brown,' I explained. 'I believe you're expecting me?'

The nun glanced towards my stomach, and then nodded without smiling. 'I'm Sister Teresa,' she said shortly. 'Come inside.' The frost in her voice was almost palpable, a sharp and chilly tremor cutting through the still September air. I lowered my eyes as I pulled my suitcase over the threshold, acutely aware of her penetrating and disapproving gaze.

The door shut, and a sepulchral gloominess descended as she had me follow her through one of the panelled doors off the hallway into a high-ceilinged room. It was sparsely furnished, with a large oak desk and chair in the centre and a cabinet containing books and several statues. I couldn't make out any of the titles, but I imagined the books would be religious. I certainly recognised the statues, good Catholic girl that I was: they were of the Child of Prague and St Anthony.

Her habit swishing audibly, Sister Teresa strode over to the desk, where a stern-faced nun sat; the wall behind her held a picture of the Sacred Heart. As with everything else in the room – human or otherwise – it seemed to be there specifically to judge me.

'Reverend Mother, this is Angela Brown,' Sister Teresa announced respectfully. Reverend Mother began reading from a collection of papers while I stood silently, my case parked beside me, on the edge of a worn patterned rug. I had spent my entire school life in the company of nuns, and I felt like I was back at school now – only this was so much worse.

Finally she raised her head and addressed me. 'Can you confirm your name?' she asked crisply. 'And your baby's due date?'

I did, and was surprised to find my voice had all but disappeared on the long bus journey. I cleared my throat. She glared.

'And I also need to know the name of the person we should contact in case of emergency,' she continued. 'Will that be your mother, Mrs Phillips?'

'Yes,' I confirmed, my voice still small. 'That's correct.'

'Right,' she said, closing the file and fixing me with another disapproving look. 'Now that's done, Sister Teresa will take you straight up to your room. You'll be sharing with Mary, another expectant mother.' She stood up now. 'She has a due date close to yours,' she finished. 'Now come along.'

I followed her along a passage to another, smaller staircase, struggling now with my heavy case. I didn't need to worry about keeping up: Sister Teresa, for all her presence, was actually quite frail and was finding the stairs as challenging as I was. After climbing two flights and walking single file along a thin upstairs passage to the very end, we reached the door to the room in question.

The room was tiny – no bigger than twelve feet by ten – and furnished very sparsely. It held two hospital-style beds, each of which had a hospital-style locker, in which it was clear we'd need to keep all our possessions. Except for a chipped washbasin under a sash window framed by faded curtains and a wooden chair, there was nothing else in the room.

Nothing, that is, bar a delicate-looking girl, who had fair hair and slightly protruding front teeth. She'd been sitting on the left-hand bed, writing a letter, but had leapt to her feet, startled, as we entered. Though smiling shyly at me, she looked flustered, which wasn't surprising: Sister Teresa hadn't announced our arrival. As I would soon find out, the nuns *never* knocked.

'Mary, this is Angela Brown,' Sister Teresa explained. Then, to me, 'Angela, this is Mary Bourke. You two will be sharing a room until your babies are delivered.'

What would happen after that, she didn't say. She moved aside to let me pass her and enter the room properly. I smelt dampness. Mary smiled again and gestured towards the other, empty bed. She was petite, and wore a pinafore-style dress, underneath which was a hand-knitted jumper. In contrast to my intentionally well-disguised bump, hers, to my eye, looked enormous. What a relief it would be, I decided on seeing it, to give my own poor, squashed baby some room to move about. I'd been so fearful for so long about the damage I might be doing that when the baby had first kicked me, as well as a wave of profound relief, I felt it might have been in angry protest.

'Now, Mary,' Sister Teresa continued, in a voice that, though directed at Mary, was also designed to make it clear to me that I mustn't assume she was as frail as she appeared. It occurred to me that my new roommate probably knew it already. 'I'd be grateful if you could kindly show Angela the bathroom, and familiarise her with the timetable of our daily routine here. Once you're done, and Angela has unpacked her belongings, will you please bring her back down, so I can show her the work she'll be doing while she's here.'

She turned to me then. 'You'll find me in the milk kitchen, which is where you'll be working. Mary will be able to show you where that is.'

I'd never heard of a milk kitchen before, and immediately an image of a cattle stall, complete with a row of placid Friesians, came to mind. It was an image that in other circumstances might have made me smile. A smile didn't reach my lips now, though. It didn't dare.

Mary nodded and promised we wouldn't be long. With a short nod in return, Sister Teresa swept out.

Once we were alone together, the air no longer chilled by the nun's frosty presence, I felt inexplicably calm and relieved. In anticipation, this place had seemed such a terrifying prospect, yet now I was here it felt as if a weight had lifted. This was the first time, I realised, that I was in the company of someone who was in exactly the same dire straits as I was; someone who could not only sympathise but also empathise with me; someone who knew what I was going through because she was going through it too. It felt such a relief that I could be honest about my situation. At last I had a confidante, and so did Mary.

She sat down again as I hauled my suitcase onto my bed. I winced. My back hurt from lugging it for so long. 'Have you come far?' she asked, putting her pen and pad to one side.

I shook my head. 'Not very,' I replied. 'Just a few miles on the bus. I've been staying with a friend since ... well, since all this happened.'

I turned to smile back, as I opened up the case and began sorting out the contents. I'd been given a list of what to pack for the baby. As well as my few maternity clothes, nightwear and toiletries, I'd packed terry nappies, vests and some nighties and booties that, touchingly, my close friends from work had contributed. I also had matinée jackets, knitted by my sister-in-law Emmie, and a cold-weather outfit that I'd seen in a shop in Elm Park and bought in white, as I didn't know the baby's sex.

On the top of the pile was the intricate knitted shawl that Emmie had made for when the baby was to be handed over for adoption. Seeing it again now made me start. Like the baby, it would not be mine for very long. I quickly put all thoughts of what was to come out of my mind, as they reminded me just how soon I'd be giving birth. It felt scarily real now that I was here. I reached to open my locker and began filling the tiny space inside with my possessions.

'How about you?' I asked Mary, whose accent made me suspect she'd travelled a great deal further than I had.

'Oh, a long way,' she confirmed. 'I've come from Ireland. Wexford. Do you know it, by any chance?'

I nodded. 'I've not been there, but I have family in County Waterford. My mother comes from there. You're right; it *is* a long way,' I said.

She nodded glumly. 'It feels like it, to be sure. No one at home knows I'm here. I told them I was coming to London to find work.' This wouldn't have been an unusual scenario: the economic situation in Ireland was pretty grim in the sixties, and lots of young Irish girls came to England to get work. 'So now I'm a waitress,' she told me, smiling ruefully, lifting the pages of carefully written untruths from beside her on the bedcover. 'I've been telling them all about it – what a grand job it is.' The smile was still there, but it was a bleak one.

'So you've not told *anyone*?' I asked her. 'Is there no one you've confided to at all?' I couldn't imagine how isolating and horrible that must be. Thank goodness I had Emmie and a couple of dear work friends to support me.

'Not a soul. I dared not. Can you imagine the consequences?'

I nodded. I could. To be pregnant and unmarried in England was bad enough, but for a young Irish Catholic girl it was unthinkable. She would be shunned, unmarriageable, thought the lowest of the low. The level of hatred and vitriol against young unmarried mothers there was well known. It was something that could disgrace a girl for life.

'Except the father,' she added, her expression darkening further. 'He knows, all right. But he's married. And he already has two children to support. So what can *he* do to help me?' She sounded like she was reciting the very words he'd said to her.

'I'm so sorry,' I said. 'That's awful . . .'

'Not so awful as getting pregnant, let me tell you, and only *then* finding out he'd got a family.' She sounded and looked distraught now, her eyes filling with tears. I wasn't sure if I should stop what I was doing and go and comfort her; I nearly did, but something about her body language told me not to. She pulled a piece of tissue from the sleeve of her jumper and dabbed angrily with it.

'I'm a fool, is what I am,' she said. 'Blind. Just plain blind.' She pushed the tissue away back out of sight and spread her hands. 'But aren't we all sometimes? I loved him. I *still* love him – much good it'll do me. But mostly I'm just so homesick.'

'I'm sure you are.'

'And terrified, of course. Can you imagine if someone finds out where I really am?' she asked again. There was a look of real fear on her face.

'But no one *can*,' I reassured her. 'I mean, I don't *know* that, obviously, but I don't see how anyone could, not if you don't tell them.' I squashed all my things I could into the locker. The rest – the baby things, which I wouldn't need for a while yet – could stay in the case.

'I know. I'm probably worrying too much. It just gets to you, this, doesn't it? But what about you?' she asked. 'What about *your* baby's father?'

Peter, I thought. I didn't even think of him in those terms. And why would I? My baby and I were in this on our own. 'I took a risk,' I told her. 'I was silly. I just never thought ...' I didn't need to finish the sentence. She was already nodding.

'And has he supported you? Are you with him still?'

I shook my head. 'He doesn't even know,' I said. 'We're not together. It wasn't serious. By the time I found out I was pregnant, we'd already split up. So I suppose I don't have all that to deal with.'

'Oh, you've more than enough to deal with. We *all* have,' she said. 'But we must hurry.' She jumped up. 'There's room for your case underneath your bed – just, I think. Here, let me help you. There you go. Sister Teresa will be waiting, and she doesn't like to be kept waiting. I can show you the bathroom as we go.'

'How long have you been here?' I asked, as we left the little room – my new home – and retraced our steps along the corridor.

'A week,' she said. 'A very *long* week.'

'And what job have they given you?'

'Cleaning,' she said. And then she grinned at me. 'So whatever the state of our souls, at least the floors shine.'

'How is it? I mean, generally. Is it as bad here as it seems?'

We'd turned a corner now. Mary put her hand on an adjacent doorknob. 'You've experience of nuns?'

I nodded. 'Oh, yes. I went to a convent school.'

'So think that, only more so, since we're all in a state of mortal sin now and must atone. Anyway, *voilà*. Grand, don't you think?'

I peered in. As with everything here, the bathroom was basic. A large basin, a toilet and a chipped enamelled cast-iron bath sat on a black and white tiled floor, surrounded by plain grey-white walls. You could feel the cold coming off them. I touched one. It was icy. The bathroom was shared, Mary told me, by about twenty of us.

'So it's a bit of a scrum in the mornings,' she said. 'Not that anyone wants to linger, as you can imagine.'

We then returned down a back staircase to the ground floor. Here we took a route through another maze of passages until we came to the milk kitchen and, as promised, Sister Teresa. She was standing by a long Formica worktop, filling baby feeding bottles with formula milk, wearing a large apron and starched cotton over-sleeves to protect her habit from splashes.

'Now then,' she said to me, once Mary had been dismissed and had returned to our room. 'As Mary's probably told you, all the girls who come here have duties assigned to them, and you will be working here in the milk kitchen. Starting tomorrow.'

Sister Teresa then went on to describe, in dizzying detail, the nature of the duties I'd be expected to carry out, which sounded like they would dominate most of the waking hours of every day. Pregnant mothers, who did not yet have babies to care for, could be under no illusions. 'Here in the convent,' Sister Teresa explained, 'you will be expected to work just as hard as we do; to rise early and use the day productively just as we do; to attend mass and to ask the Lord's forgiveness.' I noticed she didn't tag 'just as we do' on the end of that last one.

Apart from the endless standing, which was tiring because my legs and ankles became increasingly sore and swollen, I soon learned I had got off reasonably lightly. Some girls had been assigned much more punishing duties, such as working in the laundry, where vast quantities of dirty terry nappies were laundered each day. The nappies had to be transferred, steaming and soaking, from the huge washing vats to be rinsed and then spun in the enormous dryer. For anyone this would be hard physical work, but for girls at such an advanced stage of pregnancy it was exhausting.

'Your day begins directly after breakfast,' Sister Teresa explained now, as she showed me the various items of paraphernalia that would become my only companions for much of the day. 'You'll come in here, and first wash the previous night's bottles and teats, then put them in the steriliser, here. After that, you'll make up the three feeds for the daytime and, that done, you'll wash down the worktops and floor.'

'How many babies are here?' I ventured to ask her, as there seemed to be so many bottles.

'Around ten,' she said crisply. 'More or less. It varies. And cleanliness is key,' she reminded me. 'You have sole responsibility for the milk kitchen, Angela, and cleanliness is paramount at all times. That is why proper sterilisation is vital. This is a job that requires great attention to hygiene. Do you understand that?'

She sounded like she assumed I'd know nothing about hygiene, having not known how to resist the evils of the flesh. I assured her I did and that I would take the greatest of care.

'You then have further duties after supper,' she added, 'when you'll return here to make up a second batch of bottles: those for the night-time and early morning feeds.'

As I stood there, trying hard to take everything in so as not to attract even more of her disapproval, I imagined filling one of those neatly ranked bottles and feeding my own baby from it. I felt completely out of my depth. This was a world I hadn't any experience of and it frightened me. Everything about it felt alien. Yet, at the same time, the idea made me feel unexpectedly maternal. I was trying so hard to put it all out of my mind, but I had a baby growing inside me, kicking me and squirming, and making its presence felt – my own *child*. I didn't want to think about the baby, because it was going to be taken away from me. But seeing the little bottles triggered something inside me, and I couldn't seem to shake off the thought of that future parting.

That first evening at Loreto Convent is a blur now. I recall a supper, at around 5.30, of watery scrambled eggs, and meeting lots of other girls, all pink cheeked and lumbering and anxious of expression, all in the same desperate plight. Though I met new mothers, too, and could hear regular mewling cries, I remember being shocked that I hadn't seen any babies. Where were they? Why weren't they there?

'Because they spend every moment of their lives in the nursery,' Mary told me once we were back up in our room again, getting ready for bed. 'On their own.'

'That's awful,' I said, genuinely surprised. 'Aren't the mothers allowed to bring them out?'

'Heavens, no!'

I was shocked again. I'd had a picture, insofar as I'd had a picture of anything, of the new mothers sitting together, feeding their infants and chatting, helping one another, comparing notes. 'So do they go to them, then? In the nursery?' I asked her.

Mary's expression made it clear that even after a week she was already much more clued up than I was. 'They are allowed in *only* to feed them and change them,' she said. 'Though no breastfeeding; breastfeeding isn't allowed here. And it's forbidden to go into the nursery at any other time. Oh, and they're not to be taken out of the nursery, either. One of the girls did that last week. Well, I think that's what she intended. She got no further than the doorway, and she got such a vicious dressing down, you wouldn't believe. No, they're never allowed out – not till they leave here.'

'What, *never*?' I gasped, as the picture in my head dissolved away. However little I'd allowed myself to wonder how things might be before my baby was adopted, spending time with it, nursing it, cuddling it, being with it were all things I'd taken as given – but I was wrong.

Mary was shaking her head.

Once again it struck me: I hadn't seen a single baby. 'But why would that be?'

'Oh, they'll have you think it's so we don't get too attached to them – or them to us, for that matter. But I'm thinking having to listen to them crying themselves to sleep all the time is another a part of the punishment.'

'That's awful,' I said again. 'And so cruel. It's not the babies' fault, is it? Why are *they* being punished? They didn't ask to be born into these circumstances, did they?'

But as soon as I thought that, the guilt just weighed heavier.

Whose fault was it that my baby was going to be born in this grim place? All mine.

Mary looked so frightened that night. So frightened and so lonely, kneeling beside her little bed, so far from home and loved ones, saying prayers to a God she must have felt had abandoned her.

The lights went out moments after – 9 p.m. was the curfew – and I felt shattered, as world-weary as it was possible to be. But there was also the cruel irony of feeling so young at the same time, of lying in the blackness, the old building groaning and creaking around me, and feeling like a naughty girl back in my convent school being snapped at for some minor misdemeanour or other, feeling powerless and insignificant and vulnerable and ill thought of by cold, distant nuns.

My last thoughts were of my unborn baby's father, of my exciting life in London, of the burgeoning career I'd had to flee from and of the night I'd spent with Peter, having foolishly fallen for charms so fleeting that they'd soon melted away. Nothing could have been in starker contrast to the position in which I now found myself. What had I been *thinking*? I felt a deepening despair and a sense that I had ruined everything.

I pulled my knees up towards my tummy and tried not to cry. My nose inches from the cold wall, I clasped my arms around my body and felt the warm bulk of my baby, gently stirring inside me, blissfully ignorant of what was to come. An unbearable loneliness descended and engulfed me. I'd never felt so wretched.

I'd made the most terrible mistake of my life. And now I was going to have to pay for it.

Chapter Three

'Mary! Angela!'

Sister Teresa's voice was so shrill it would slice through the heaviest of slumbers, but when she rapped on the bedroom door at seven o'clock sharp the next morning, I'd already been awake for some time. I'd listened to the small sounds of sleep Mary was making in the other bed, but for me the fitful slumber that had finally claimed me had been interrupted at intervals all night. By the movement of my baby? By some sudden noise? By the sound of crying? I didn't know. But lying in the blackness in that unfamiliar bed, the dark hours before dawn had seemed endless.

Unsurprisingly, since we always shy away from awful truths, it had taken a while for me to accept that I really was pregnant. I'd started my periods at the age of eleven, and was given just one sex education lecture by my mother. It consisted of six words: 'never let a man touch you'. This had naturally conjured up all sorts of astonishing visions, none of which was remotely relevant to the situation I was in now.

I had done that classic thing: I'd been entirely swept up in the moment. Those words, uttered all those years back – and never repeated, much less qualified – were as nothing. They might just as well have never been said.

By the time I made the appointment with the company doctor (my then employers, like many of their kind in the City, retained one to look after the health and welfare of their staff), I'd missed three periods. And though I knew, deep down, that I was clutching at straws, still I clung to anything that might counter reality. Perhaps I was suffering from some obscure illness? Maybe I was about to make medical history.

It was a vain hope. I knew it was, too, for I'd already taken action. Only a few days before, I'd confided in a friend and she'd given me the name and number of an abortionist.

Clasping the slip of paper she'd given me as if it were a clutch of priceless diamonds, I'd slipped my coat on, left my offices and made my way through the hurrying midday throng to Eastcheap, where I knew there was a public phone box in the Post Office. I dialled the number with urgent fingers, feeling tongue-tied and anxious. Where did you start when you were making such a confession?

'Yes?' came the greeting, six or seven rings in. It was a woman's voice – sharp. I hardly knew where to begin.

'I've been given your number,' I said. 'I'm pregnant, you see, and I—'

The woman didn't let me get any further. 'What was the date of your last period?' she wanted to know.

I told her.

There wasn't even a second's hesitation. 'Then I'm sorry, but I can't help you,' she said.

This left me momentarily speechless. What? Just like that? It sounded so final, so brutal.

'But my friend said you might be able to do something even so.' I could feel my throat tightening as tears of frustration began to well in my eyes.

'I'm sorry,' the woman said again. 'But really, I can't.'

'But couldn't you just see me at least? Examine me? I'm sure—'

'*No.*' Her voice was emphatic. 'You are much too far gone for any sort of intervention. Your friend shouldn't have told you any such thing. If you'd come to me earlier, then perhaps ...'

Oh, God. Why *hadn't* I? 'I'm not completely certain about the dates,' I tried desperately. 'It might be that—'

'Look, I really can't do anything for you,' she said again. 'It would be much too dangerous, too likely to involve complications. And if something went wrong, and you had to go to hospital—'

'I wouldn't care! Anything would be better than—'

'No, *you* might not care, but I would. You must see that. Abortion is illegal, as you well know. So the next thing would be that the police would become involved. So where would that leave me? Where would it leave all the others who might need my help?'

'Please!' I was crying now. 'You must be able to do *something*!'

'I can't. I'm so sorry. I just can't.'

'But if you can't help me, what am I going to *do*? Please, I'm desperate!'

But then I realised I was talking into a void. She had obviously disconnected the call. And she'd been right to do so.

The company doctor sat me down and told me I was already four months pregnant. I was almost halfway down a road I had no choice but to go down now, and at its end lay a terrifying unknown.

Travelling home from work that evening, walking past all the rows and rows of identical bungalows, with only the occasional 'room in the roof' breaking the monotony of the dreary land-scape, I knew with that crushing news my fate was sealed. Whatever happened now, I was going to have this baby. And then? I simply had no idea.

When I got home, both my mother and stepfather, Sam, were there to greet me, sitting like judge and jury, frowning. It was immediately obvious that they would not like the verdict: I could see it in their eyes.

My mother, like most mothers back then, kept an eye on my periods. I'd been making excuses for the lack of them ever since I'd missed the first one, ironically only a day after finishing with Peter. It had been a very short infatuation, which ended once I realised, again during an evening at the Ilford Palais, that I wasn't the only one to fall for his skill at charming women.

I'd had a urinary infection just after missing that period and my mother had marched me to the local GP. He'd prescribed antibiotics, and the infection had cleared, but when the next period also failed to arrive, she marched me straight back.

This time I was given a single pill to take, which he assured us would bring on my period. If it didn't happen, he advised, then

I must go back again. It was about now that alarm bells began ringing for us both, and my mother began questioning me, over and over again, about whether there was any way I could be pregnant. I denied it emphatically, citing the urinary infection as the only reason I could think of for my period's non-appearance. All the while I was in a state of growing terror.

The days passed. When, despite the pill, there was no sign of the period, my mother, now quite agitated, changed her mind about going to the GP. I couldn't go back, she informed me, because the neighbours might find out; one of them worked as a receptionist at the surgery.

Now, standing before my mother and stepfather, I cursed my stupidity. If only I'd acted sooner. What a fool I'd been.

'I'm pregnant,' I said. Because what else was there to say?

My mother's hand flew to her mouth.

'Dear God,' she said. 'Jesus, Mary and Joseph! Oh, Angela, what have you *done*?'

Since the question was rhetorical, I didn't answer it. I couldn't meet her gaze either. I could just see Sam's face, out of the corner of my eye, and that was all I needed to gauge his expression. At some point, much later, I felt sure he'd tell my mother that this was only what he'd expected from a girl like me.

'What have you done?' she said again. She clasped her hands together, as if in prayer. 'Dear God,' she said again. 'What have I done to deserve this? Oh, Angela, you have sinned. You have done *such* a bad thing! How on earth are we going to . . . Oh, this is a *nightmare*! Oh, *Angela*!' I could feel her eyes boring into me. 'What are we going to *do*?' I looked up now, my cheeks burning.

She raised a finger and jabbed it towards me. 'You do know you can't stay here, don't you?'

I gasped. What was she saying? She couldn't mean that, surely? 'But where else will I go?'

'I don't know yet, but we'll have to get something arranged – and quickly. We can't have the neighbours finding out about this.'

'But where?' I said again, feeling panicky. Would she really throw me out? *Could* she?

'You'll need to find lodgings,' she went on. 'Somewhere you can stay, well away from here, until, well, until it can all be dealt with.'

I looked at her, aghast, as the grim reality of my situation became clearer. *Until it can all be dealt with*. I could hardly bear to think about what that meant. 'So should I look in the newspaper?' I finally managed to say. 'Try to find a room to rent? Where?'

She exhaled heavily, making it clear that my suggestion – effectively, that she intended to put me out on the street – was further evidence of my irresponsibility. 'You might have thought of that, Angela, while you were doing what you were doing!' She cast around the room as if she might find the answer somewhere within it. Then her hand went to her forehead again.

'Which of your friends could you ask?' she said eventually. 'Is there someone from your office you could rent a room from?' She looked sharply at me again. 'Angela, you *know* you can't stay here.'

'But—'

'You *have* to leave.' Her voice was high with anxiety now – even panic at the thought I might be about to beseech her to let me stay, to throw myself at her feet and beg. But I wouldn't do that. I could see it would be pointless. 'Only temporarily,' she added. 'But before anyone finds out.' Her tone softened slightly. 'Angela, you *do* see that, don't you?'

I did see that, I told her. And by now I did, because I'd had it drummed into me for half my life. How could she possibly let me stay when I'd committed a mortal sin? What worse disgrace could ever befall a Catholic family? I hung my head again. I felt more dreadful already than any amount of her shouting could have made me. I had let her and my entire family down. I *knew* that. Yes, I was shocked at how forcibly I'd been told there were no options, but I'd brought it on myself, so what else could I expect? I felt so disappointed in myself, and so full of regret. I also felt afraid, because now I had nowhere to go and absolutely no idea what was to become of me.

From that moment on, things became very strained between us. My mother simply couldn't disguise her disgust and dismay that her only daughter had committed the ultimate sin. I knew I had to get away as soon as possible, because every day I stayed, there was a greater risk of my secret coming out.

Thankfully, when I went into work the next day, and confided in the closest of my colleagues, they were sympathetic and supportive. Though here, too, there was bad news. I'd expected it, of course, but it didn't make it any easier to swallow.

'You know you'll have to leave, don't you?' my boss, Bunty, explained. Unlike my mother's, her tone was gentle and reassuring. 'And sooner rather than later,' she added, squeezing my arm. 'Because that way you can, in all probability, come back.'

I brightened a little. 'I can?' This was something I hadn't expected.

'Absolutely,' she said. 'You're a skilled member of staff. It would make no sense for us to lose you. But it has to be quickly, before anyone senior finds out. If they do, you'll be shunned and that'll definitely be the end of it – bye, bye Angela. Honestly,' she said, 'they'll treat you as no better than a prostitute, especially the men. But if you leave on some other pretext – an extended holiday, say – it's up to you. What do you think? Then you can return after you've had it, and continue as before.'

'How about Italy?' I asked. I'd been to Italy on holiday the year before and had fallen in love with it, so much so that I'd immediately signed up for evening classes in Italian. I'd gone with three other friends – all good Catholic girls like myself – and we'd spent a glorious fortnight in the pretty seaside resort of Laigueglia. I suggested it to Bunty. 'I could say I was going on an extended trip to Laigueglia, I suppose, to improve my fluency by working there this time. Would that do?'

Bunty thought that would work perfectly. It would make the subterfuge on my return that bit easier to deflect. And so it was agreed: I was heading to Europe for a while. I handed in my week's notice and left.

But there was still the problem of getting temporary accommodation. Now I was no longer going to work every day, my mother became even more anxious to move me out. What if someone saw me and wondered why I wasn't going to work? So the neighbours, too, were told the story of my upcoming trip to Italy. Thankfully, I didn't have to dodge their enquiries about my plans for long, as within the week I had somewhere new to live.

In this, also, I was lucky to have had such wonderful friends at work: my friend and colleague June, after okaying it with her husband – another Peter, ironically – offered to let me live in the spare room in their house in Elm Park. In return I'd pay a small rent and help out with the household chores, and I couldn't have been more grateful. I still am.

June was the antithesis of almost everyone else around me at that time. While the whole world, it seemed, stood in damning judgement over me, June had been the friend I'd been able to call on for support and advice. It had been she who had given me the abortionist's number, and had earlier given me potions to try. She was from Bow, in the East End, and as down to earth and colourful as I was reserved and self-effacing. She was pretty and glamorous, and was a model in her spare time. She was also streetwise: her extended family were the sort of people who get tagged 'likeable rogues', selling things that 'dropped off the back of a lorry'.

Just as June didn't judge me, I didn't judge her. She was a rock, a tower of strength and a true friend in a time of crisis. It was impossible to thank her enough or properly repay her for what she did for me, and I felt I never could, even though we stayed in touch for many, many years, even after she emigrated to Australia.

Despite all this kindness, I was terrified. Where on earth would I get a job so I could pay June my rent? Who would employ a pregnant, unmarried nineteen year old? And where would I go to have my baby? I had no idea. Still more worrying was what would happen once the baby was born. Where would we live? How would I manage? Back then there was no social security in place. Would I be destitute with a newborn? How could I not be? Would the authorities take it away from me?

And in all of this, the one person whom I'd normally depend on most was completely unable to help me. My mother could talk to no one – ask no questions, get no advice – because if she did, then the secret would be out.

It was then that the bleakness of my situation became real.

'How was your night?' Mary asked me, interrupting my reverie. Her voice was soft, but it echoed in the sparsely furnished room.

'I didn't sleep very much,' I admitted, returning her shy smile. 'But it's difficult to get comfortable when you're this big, isn't it? Even in the most comfortable bed.'

Mary grinned and pulled the covers back, then swung her legs to the floor. 'And these beds are definitely not that,' she answered ruefully.

This small quip was at odds with the tone of the morning, as we left the freezing bedroom and made our way down, along with the other girls, to queue for the bathroom, the cold air swirling unpleasantly around our bare legs. I would soon understand there was a reason for the quiet, for the way the girls, myself included, seemed locked in their own worlds. It was due, I decided, probably to that sense of waking up in the home every morning and being reminded anew of the terrible situation we were in, every bit as much as it was to tiredness.

The bathroom was gloomy and uninviting, the early morning light diffused by its frosted window. Being a convent, it was important that no one have the chance to see us naked – somewhat ironic, given the condition we were in. It was also very cold (soon it would become even colder) so, just as Mary had told me, no one was inclined to hang around.

Once we were washed, we sped back to our bedrooms to dress. I had a selection of maternity clothes – smocks and elasticated waist skirts – that June's neighbour, a lovely Irish lady called Marie, had kindly dug out and let me have. Then Mary and I headed down to breakfast.

The dining room, like every other room I'd seen so far, was dingy in aspect and minimally furnished. In this case, it was dominated by a long, thin refectory table, accessorised with wooden chairs of all ages and styles, probably assembled and repaired and then replaced over many years. Like the nuns, they looked worn out and creaky with age.

You could sit anywhere, though breakfast was not a leisurely affair: it was designed to set you up for the day's work, not as an accompaniment to idle chitchat. Just as when we had gone down to the bathroom, I got a strong sense that talk was discouraged.

Such talk as there was, from what I could make out that first morning, was quiet and mostly centred on the mothers' unhappiness and stress at finding their babies crying when they went in to do the first feed of the day.

'Lots of the mothers miss breakfast altogether,' Mary told me, 'which is why it's half empty in here now. Sure, they're hungry, but they need that extra hour's sleep a lot more – or so I'm told, and I don't doubt it.'

Neither did I.

The food was simple and wholesome: a selection of cereals, sometimes porridge. There was also a toaster so the girls could make themselves toast if they wanted. But the main thing I noticed round the table that morning was that a definite hierarchy existed in Loreto Convent: pregnant girls and mothers each tended to stick to their own. There was our group, bewildered, naive and full of fear; then another of those mothers who'd made it to breakfast – there would be more at lunch and tea. They looked hollowed-eyed and whey-faced, on the edge of exhaustion and sad. They were the ones whose journeys were nearing an end, and for whom the future, now they'd brought their babies into the world, must have seemed very bleak.

There were five nuns in the convent, all of them different ages, but uniformly stern and impatient: Reverend Mother Sylvester, Sister Teresa – undoubtedly the oldest, Sister Veronica, Sister Michael and Sister Roc. None showed an iota of affection, so there was no 'softer' option. As my job was in the milk kitchen and Sister Teresa's was the care of the babies, I would be taking my orders mostly from her.

And she seemed to like to give them. She appeared, habit swishing purposefully, within what seemed like seconds of sitting down to eat. 'Are you done, Angela?' she asked me, in her high, reedy voice. 'Because there's work to be done. This is not a hotel! These bottles won't be making up themselves, you know.'

I wanted to point out that I'd never considered it to be one, but I swallowed my words along with the last spoonful of my cereal and, having established that my dirty crockery would be another girl's responsibility – 'put it there, girl!' – hurried after her out of the dining room.

The milk kitchen didn't really resemble a kitchen at all. It was a small space, and apart from having a sink and a draining board, and the long Formica worktop, it was more reminiscent of a large pantry. It would be in this tiny space that I would spend the majority of my days till I went to hospital to have my baby.

Sister Teresa gave me a handwritten list, on which was noted the name of each mother who was staying at the convent and the amount of Cow and Gate formula milk her baby was supposed to have at each feed. As I looked at the list of names and their accompanying allocation, reality hit me hard: I was going to have a baby and one day soon that baby would be on this list. Except it wouldn't be; just my name would be on the list. My baby, who by then would be very much alive, would be a non-person, not even granted a name of his or her own.

Sister Teresa, who would spend much of my first couple of days hovering, had been very clear on one thing when I arrived at the convent, and made a point of restating it now. 'On no account,' she said, gesturing to the list in my hand, 'are you to deviate from the amounts stated on this list, Angela. Not by so much as a drop, you understand? Accuracy is paramount.'

'Okay,' I said. After all, it didn't look that difficult to measure.

'And you mustn't listen to anyone who tells you otherwise. Anyone, you understand? You'll have mothers coming in—' Here she narrowed her tiny eyes and looked as if she were about to disclose something dreadful. 'And they'll be asking for more. Just a drop here and a drop there – but you're not to give it. No exceptions. Understand?'

I would soon find out that this was a regular occurrence: mothers furtively slipping down to the milk kitchen to ask if they could have just a little more. And these requests, I would come to learn, weren't unreasonable. Feeding times were short, and as regimented as everything else was, so it was quite common that not all of the babies finished their feeds in the allotted time. Which made it only fair, their mothers argued, for them to have a bit more to make up for what they'd not had.

'Wait till you have a baby of your own,' one said crossly to me one day. 'Then perhaps you'll understand what it's like.'

I didn't dare deviate from what I'd been told, though – not that first day and not in all my time there. It was made clear to me that there would be serious consequences if I were caught, which I would be, as Sister Teresa was at pains to point out: she would be checking the bottles regularly.

Work continued without respite till a gong sounded for lunch. A strange and mournful noise that seemed not of its time, it would come to represent the ceaseless toil so relentlessly that eventually I hated the sound.

The routine in the milk kitchen was straightforward. Consulting the list, I made up the required number of bottles before transferring them to metal jugs filled with hot water, as I'd been shown. Each mother had her own jug, which had her name written on it. Once the feeds were made, I transferred the jugs to a big tray, which I then took into the nursery ready for the next scheduled feed.

It was unforgettable going into the nursery that very first time. The nursery was another long room, on the ground floor, with the same dingy curtains as elsewhere and about twenty cots in a horseshoe shape around the edge of it. Between each cot, which bore a tag stating 'baby of' and the mother's name, was a small locker and a chair placed there for feeding. Along half of one wall, before the first cot in the horseshoe, was a waist-height level surface on which mothers could change and clean their babies. I'd never seen one, but if I imagined a Dickensian orphanage, this would have been what sprang to mind.

Though I didn't know it on the first day, I quickly realised that specific cots weren't reserved for the duration of a child's stay. The opposite was true: the cot at the far end of the line was for the newest baby, and the cot nearest the door was for the oldest child – the infant next due to leave. The babies would move up through the cots until they occupied that final position. It was reminiscent of lambs going to slaughter.

The babies were crying, and crying lustily, when I entered. The noise was ear-splitting, piercing. A glance around the room soon confirmed why: almost all of them were wailing. I could see only two that weren't a part of the grim cacophony; they were either too exhausted or too acclimatised to the constant racket to stay awake.

There were no mothers to tend to them, to soothe their fractious bawling, since mothers, as Mary had already told me, were strictly forbidden from entering the nursery at any time other than feeding and changing times. This rule was so rigidly enforced that few girls ever dreamt of defying it. I thought how hard it must be to be a new mother and know you were forbidden from comforting your own child. I knew I wouldn't have to wonder what it felt like for very long, though. I put the tray down carefully on the long counter and quickly made my way out with the empties.

Back in the quiet and solitude of the milk kitchen, I set about the washing and sterilising without delay. It would soon be time to make up the next batch of bottles, as per the instructions on my sheet. It was a long job, hot and smelly, with the scent of the stale milk pricking my nostrils. I noticed a number of the bottles hadn't been fully drained, and wondered again at those babies' anguished cries.

By late morning I was done, and ready to prepare the next feeds, my ankles already complaining and pressing hotly against my shoes. As I untied the strings of my apron and tugged the white elasticated protective sleeves from my arms, I surveyed the list and the ranks of upside-down bottles in the steriliser.

It was shocking, the contrast between the here and now and the recent past. Just a few short months ago I'd been working at a job I loved in the City, and a typical morning would mean a few hours immersed in my work at my desk. I was a code translator, a job I found absorbing and fascinating, as I charted the progress of cargo all over the world. Charting the ships' movements, deciphering the complex codes that tracked their journeys – it might have been an office job, but it was endlessly stimulating. Knowing there might be a chance to go back to it was a crumb of real comfort. But the gulf between here and there seemed vast now, as if I had been plucked from the modern world and deposited in Edwardian times.

I wondered what my former colleagues might be doing right now: sharing a companionable lunch, no doubt, catching up on gossip. And here was I, the victim of my own stupid naivety, alone in a tiny room, peeling off a pair of heavy rubber gloves, the all-pervasive smell of Milton fluid around me, in charge of spooning powdered formula into baby bottles.

The only other thing that gave me even the smallest consolation was the fact that my beloved father, who'd died when I was fourteen, was no longer here to witness his daughter's fall from grace. Peter might have passed muster on superficial examination, but to my great shame I knew I did not.

Chapter Four

My father had met my mother in a restaurant in London in 1928. She'd been working there as a waitress – a real one, on this occasion – after recently moving to England from Ireland with her sisters.

Both my parents bore the scars of unhappy childhoods. My father's mother died when he was just three months old, her tragic death attributed to complications at his birth. Following this, and unable to forgive his infant son for his wife's demise, my grandfather virtually ignored him, and he was entrusted to the care of the housekeeper until his enlistment in the army, aged fourteen.

My mother's childhood was similarly full of tragedy. The middle of three sisters, she was born in County Waterford in Ireland, and lost her own mother when she was three years old. She and her sisters were subsequently brought up by their father until his untimely death during the 1918 Spanish flu epidemic. The sisters spent the next five years in an orphanage run by nuns, and eventually came to London when my mother was sixteen.

My father was a Protestant and my mother, coming from a

devout Catholic family, understandably provoked the wrath of her relatives in Ireland for entering into a 'mixed marriage'. But they were determined and married anyway, in 1929. They set up home in Forest Gate, East London, where, in time, my father converted to Catholicism.

My earliest recollections of my childhood are always of the overwhelming love I felt for my father. I used to write little poems to him and put them in his slippers. I would wait at the gate every day for him to come home from work, and when I saw him come into sight I would run to him and throw my arms around him, bursting with excitement.

Born in October 1943, I was the third of their three children. I had two older brothers: Raymond, who was born in 1932, and John, who came along some time after, in 1939. My father's relationship with my brothers was very different to the one he had with me – particularly with Raymond, as they didn't always see eye to eye about things, and there was often friction between them. John was much quieter and shyer than Raymond. They were opposites really: John was an introvert and Raymond an extrovert. My mother was always quick to defend them, and I felt she regarded me as the culprit whenever disagreements arose among the three of us.

Looking back, I wonder if it's the case that sometimes there's a closer affinity between mothers and sons during the growing-up years, particularly in family situations such as ours, in which I, the youngest child and a girl, was undoubtedly the apple of my father's eye. As I got older, it was also obvious that there was a big contrast between my mother's life as a young woman and the life she perceived I was having at the same point. I wonder, too, if to some extent she wanted to live her life through me, to have me do all the things she hadn't been able to do and seize all the opportunities she'd missed. At the same time, she came from a religious background and a generation for whom the notion of having 'boyfriends' simply didn't exist. While my brothers were free to do what they wanted, I was constantly reminded that, as a girl, I could not. As she frequently pointed out to me, marrying as a virgin was non-negotiable. She didn't step out with a man until she was twenty-one.

Though sometimes uncertain of my mother's affection for me, as she was never demonstrative, I did feel loved and cared for growing up. If she couldn't show her love physically, she showed it in practical ways, and would give generously to us all, even if it meant going without herself.

But I cherished my relationship with my father. When I received the news that he had cancer and had less than a year to live, I felt my world collapse around me. The months that followed are indelibly etched in my memory: palliative care in the 1950s was pitifully basic and the pain and suffering he endured as he was dying was shocking. To see this kind and lovely man reduced to the physical condition of a Belsen victim was heartbreaking for us all. He died at home, aged fifty-three, in April 1958, with my mother, my brothers and me by his side. I was fourteen years old and I was devastated.

It's telling, as I looked back during those first days I spent in Loreto Convent, that my overwhelming feeling was a sense of shame about how badly I'd let my mother down. I might have railed against her; perhaps, if I'd been born two decades later, I would have. But for all the pity I felt for my own situation, I worried far more about the effect all this was having on her. It would take me a long time to understand it, because our relationship was complex, but after my father died – making her a widow at fifty-one – I'd taken on the emotional burden, either wittingly or not, of being the strong one for her.

I had had to grow up extremely quickly. Within a year of my father's death, my mother and I were alone. My brothers, both of whom were engaged when he died, had left to start new lives elsewhere: John to begin two years' national service, and Raymond and his wife to sail for a new life in South Africa.

My mother struggled to cope, emotionally, physically and financially. We were now penniless. Apart from a small insurance policy, which barely paid for his funeral, my poor father had been unable to leave us anything. For me, personally, the cruellest blow after his death was leaving my school, the Ursuline High School in Ilford, where I was enjoying a good education. My mother could simply no longer afford to pay the fees, and the whole thing was humiliating and distressing.

I'd been about to embark on my GCEs that summer, but when I had to leave school, aged only 14, it seemed a bleak future lay ahead. Subsequently, I was enrolled in a secretarial college and a new course was set for my life.

I'd brought a wedding ring with me to Loreto Convent, a cheap thing I'd bought when I moved to June's house. During most

of my pregnancy I had no need to lie about my marital status.
I went to work in my new job as an audio typist at a firm of
wood preservative manufacturers in Dagenham, called
Solignum, only after squeezing myself, increasingly painfully,
into torturous foundation garments. Like Mary, I had to fashion
a story: I told them that June's house was my real home and that
I lived there with my parents. But at least no one knew I was
pregnant.

Now at the convent and hugely pregnant, it was impossible to
hide, so the ring was to cover my shame and embarrassment
when I went to my antenatal appointments. To go without it – for
people to know the truth – would be unimaginable.

It was a Friday afternoon, several days after my arrival. A few
of us had finished our duties for the day (though mine would
continue later, when I made up the last feed of the evening),
when Mary explained that we were allowed out to the shops in the
afternoons, if we asked permission and were back by 5 p.m.
sharp.

'Really?' I said. It had never occurred to me that we'd be able
to do that. Everything about the convent was so reminiscent of
a prison that the idea that it wasn't came as a shock.

She nodded. 'To buy anything personal we need – toiletries
and so on. Plus you can get eggs for breakfast there, too, if you
want to. And we tend to club together to buy treats: now you've
seen the food on offer here, you know why. We get biscuits
mostly, crisps and cakes – things like that.' She touched my arm
and pulled a face. 'Though obviously you mustn't let the nuns
see.'

So I'd slipped the ring on my finger and walked down to the village, enjoying the feeling of fresh air on my face after so many days spent entirely indoors.

The convent grounds were extensive, so it was curious, looking back, that apart from cleaning windows, washing the paintwork or sweeping up leaves, the girls never seemed to go outside. Perhaps it was because we had so little free time; perhaps it was also because strolling around a large swathe of garden seemed to be the very opposite of what we should be doing in our currently shameful state of mortal sin.

Theydon Bois was a small place, which had just a few shops that sat together in the middle of a residential area down the hill. There was a sweet shop, a chemist and a small grocer's. I'd come armed with a list of things for a few of the other girls and, when I saw the bakery, a plan to buy a cake for myself and Mary, as I'd been told the ones they sold were lovely. I also had a passion for peaches then, so I intended to get some, though they were very expensive at that time of year and would have to be just an occasional treat.

The world now took a generally dim view of me and straight away I had my first proper experience of how I was perceived. I entered the bakery and waited patiently while the lady behind the counter served the person before me, chatting in a very friendly fashion all the while, exchanging pleasantries about the late September weather. But when she turned to serve me, it seemed she took one look at my bump, and her manner changed abruptly and completely.

'Yes?' she said sharply. 'Can I help you?'

Her tone seemed to suggest she'd rather do anything but.

I pointed to the cakes – white iced buns – that I wanted. 'Yes,' I said politely. 'Two of those, please.'

She pulled a box from a stack and assembled it deftly, then picked up tongs and placed the cakes in it, side by side. 'Anything else?' she barked, placing the box on the counter.

I shook my head, handed over the money to pay and thanked her once, then again when she gave me my change.

There was another customer behind me now and, even as I spoke, the woman's eyes slid past me, her sour expression suddenly transformed. 'Ah, good afternoon!' she began cheerfully. 'What can I get for you today?' I slunk from the shop, my cheeks burning.

It was the same in the next shop I went into, the grocer's: no overt hostility, exactly, just this overwhelming sense that I was someone no one much cared to associate with. I left the shops and toiled back up the hill on heavy legs, aware of my baby squirming inside and my bags biting into my fingers.

But what else had I expected? I thought, as I walked the last few yards of the gravelled drive. The convent was imposing, both architecturally *and* symbolically. Everyone locally must have known, or figured out, what kind of occupation the nuns of the ironically named 'Franciscan Missionary of Divine Motherhood' were engaged in – at least in this branch of their missionary. There would be a steady stream of pregnant young 'wives' shopping here, of course. I was naive to suppose my ring would fool anyone.

*

With my experience of the quiet but chilly reception of some of the local businesses fresh in my mind, I resolved to learn to accept my situation. I was incarcerated in the convent – if not physically, at least emotionally – until my baby was born and I'd given it away. Then I would be allowed to slip quietly back into the life I'd led before, reintegrating into 'polite' society without anyone knowing why I'd been away.

That there was no alternative available to me was clear. I had come to accept that keeping my baby – always a dream – was something that wasn't going to happen. In fact, nothing could have been made more clear to me by my mother. As a good Catholic girl, I must do the good Catholic thing: accept the kindness of the nuns who deigned to care for us both and leave them to sort out the mess I had got myself into. Then – another thing for which I knew I must be grateful – I must give my poor child to a good Catholic family, who could care for it and bring it up properly.

Like many a girl in my situation at that time, I didn't dare question this. How could I? To mention keeping the baby as an option would have been unthinkable. As an unmarried mother I would be shunned and unable to find employment; I would therefore compound my sin by committing an innocent child to life as a destitute bastard.

So I accepted it, but it made communication with my mother difficult, because while, on the outside, I *did* accept that this was best option for my unborn infant, every fibre of my being was opposed to it. I'd spoken to my mother on the phone only sporadically since I'd gone to stay with June, and I continued to have strained and pointless conversations with her from the convent's phone at the end of the hallway.

If I was sad to be having bland conversations with a mother who knew all too well where I was, other girls had much harder circumstances to bear. Like Mary, several of the girls were living even more of a lie than I was. These were girls who'd fled situations in which no one in their families had found out what had happened, and who'd had to construct big complicated lies for their loved ones about the reason for their often sudden departure. Like Mary, they would have to write letters home, chattily talking about jobs they weren't doing, people they weren't meeting and a social life that couldn't have been further from the truth.

It was understandable, then, that thrown together as fellow outcasts, we banded together for support. And at least we had one period every day when we were left to our own devices and could relax together, away from the nuns' relentless displeasure at our very existence.

There was a common room on the ground floor, a big shabby place with a large number of lumpy mismatched chairs and an old sofa; a flickering old black and white television stood in a corner. Every evening after tea a number of us would congregate there – mostly pregnant girls rather than new mums, because the latter were generally too exhausted – to swap stories about our other lives, the ones we'd been forced to leave, and to support each other through the inevitable admissions of distress.

A lot of the conversations were about our bumps. We would discuss how big we were and how big our unborn babies might be, and we would put our hands on each other's stomachs to feel them moving. We also speculated about where we might be when our waters broke and, ignorant as most of us were about such matters, what the business of giving birth might be like.

'Did you hear about Zena?' Mary asked me one evening, a couple of weeks into my stay. Zena was one of the other pregnant girls who, unlike the rest of us, seemed more bored and fed up than distressed by her plight. There was a lot of muttering, too, about how little work she had to do and how the nuns didn't treat her like they did us. She was a model, Mary had told us, and was visited regularly by her unborn child's father. He was a wealthy married man who was supporting her through the business of dealing with their little 'inconvenience'.

'He brought round a huge bouquet of flowers this morning, by all accounts,' she said. She looked disgusted. 'And fruit. All right for some, eh? But paying her off is what it's really all about, don't you think?'

'And did you see Sister Roc around him earlier?' added Linda. 'Fawning all over him she was, like he was someone so important. When the fact is he's no better than any of us. *Worse*. Married, and with no intention of getting divorced either. Makes me sick.'

'He gives them money,' one of the other girls chipped in. 'For the convent. That's why Zena doesn't have to do half what we do. That's why she can spend her time sitting around worrying about her stretch marks. One rule for one and one rule for others. Such hypocrisy, when he's just as—'

'Hey,' called one of the girls from the other side of the common room. 'Hush up. *Ready Steady Go!* is about to start.'

We all trooped across the room to gather expectantly round

the screen. Such programmes were one of the few remaining pleasures that connected us to the lives we'd had before – even if they did also highlight how different our lives had become.

'Oh, The Beatles!' Linda squealed, as 'Twist and Shout' came on. 'I just love them; I just love them; I just love them!' She leapt up again and immediately began dancing.

'Oh, me too!' agreed another girl, getting up and pushing a couple of the armchairs out of the way to make an impromptu dance floor. I got up and helped her, and before long we were all jigging about in front of the television, the reality of our lumbering, heavily pregnant states forgotten, as for a moment at least we could forget where and who we were. When the song ended and they launched into a second number, we were so excited that we all cheered in unison, which was probably what alerted the Reverend Mother.

With our backs to the door, it took a while for us to realise she was there. It was only thanks to the enthusiastic gyrations of one girl that, one by one, we turned to see the Reverend Mother standing in the open doorway, one hand on the doorknob, the other raised in rebuke, her index finger rigid.

'Stop that at *once!*' she barked, crossing the floor, her face pink. 'What, in the name of all that's holy, do you think you're doing?!'

No one dared speak, much less move.

'Angela!' she snapped at me, causing me to jump. 'Turn that television off immediately! And you, Mary, put those chairs back where they belong! And Ann – all those cushions. Immediately!'

She stood glowering as we scurried around reassembling the

furniture. 'Have you no shame?' she said. 'Have you all forgotten why you're here?' We stood, heads hung now, short of breath and perspiring, none of us daring to reply. 'I thought so,' she said. 'And you'd do very well to. Because it's this sort of wickedness that got you all here in the first place! And it's only by the grace of God and the kindness of others that you *are* here, being cared for in your shame. How *dare* you behave in such a fashion in this place! You are here to atone, and you'd do well to remember that!'

I was standing closest to her, and could smell talc overlaid with that faint whiff of mustiness that seemed to cling tenaciously to all the nuns' habits. She looked me in the eye, and I could see how tired and old she was. 'Have you no *shame*?' she said again. Then she turned and stalked out.

It was only when we heard the door opposite bang shut that any of us dared to breathe out.

'Old witch,' Linda said.

'Hateful crone,' muttered someone else.

No one laughed. Mary burst into tears.

Lying in bed that night, I wrestled with the paradox of my situation. It seemed my world had at the same time both expanded and contracted: expanded in that I was living through such a life-changing experience, and contracted in that it was happening in this closed, claustrophobic place, where I was being treated like a child – a wicked child.

Thank God for the other girls and our growing bonds of friendship. As, in the small hours of the night, when the chattering had ceased, I realised I'd never been so alone.

Chapter Five

'Ah, Angela. There you are. I've been wanting to catch you. D'you think you could do me a really big favour?'

It was early October now and I'd gone into the nursery to collect the empty bottles after the mid-morning feed. Ann, now one of the new mothers, was still there, in the middle of changing her baby. She was at the far end, by the last cot, which was always reserved for the newest baby. I'd not spoken to her since she'd returned from the hospital, as we didn't often mix with the new mothers, but she'd always been friendly and kind to me before.

'Of course,' I said, as I made my way round to her, picking up the water jugs and empties. 'How can I help?'

'I have to go to a funeral on Friday,' she said, deftly doing up her baby daughter's nappy. She looked impossibly tiny, dark pink and so delicate, yet Ann seemed to handle her more like putty than porcelain. She cooed at her and soothed her as she folded the heavy towelling.

'I heard about that,' I said, as I reached her. 'I'm so sorry.'

She smiled wanly at me. I could see she'd been crying. 'Thanks,' she said. 'But the thing is that I'm going to be gone for most of the day, so I was wondering if you could look after Louise for me. Do her feeds – there's only two to do – and change her, of course. Would that be okay?'

I looked down at the tiny brand-new human being on the changing mat, so small and yet so unfathomable and unpredictable. It seemed impossible that in a matter of weeks I would have one of my own.

Ann lifted Louise up and pressed the tiny cheek to her own. 'She's no trouble,' she said, smiling at her daughter. 'You're an angel, aren't you?'

I picked up the last of the empty bottles, and tried to imagine myself with a baby that small and helpless in my arms. It was a huge responsibility, but at least it would be practice. 'Of course I will,' I said. 'That'll be fine.'

I'd been in the convent for three weeks and I was heavily pregnant, my enormous stomach alien in proportion to the rest of me. I'd always been slender and light-footed; now I felt swollen and exhausted, my ankles protesting painfully. Getting sufficient sleep was becoming more difficult. The baby I carried would be born soon, and it too would be one of those tiny pink beings in the nursery, dwarfed between the bars of the enormous metal cots, cots that were designed for much bigger, older babies; newborns at the convent never saw cribs.

I knew almost nothing about babies. I'd barely seen any or known any. Though Ray had two children – my niece and nephew – they'd been born in South Africa, so I'd never even met them, let alone spent time with them or cared for them. The closest member of our immediate family in England, my Auntie

Ellen, my mother's sister, had not been able to have children of her own, so I didn't have any cousins. As she too had rashly embarked on a 'mixed' marriage (her husband was a Protestant), it was forbidden for her to adopt.

I hadn't seen my Auntie Ellen since before I'd found out I was pregnant. My mother broke the news to her, and I didn't need much imagination to guess at her reaction, as she'd so often expressed her bitterness about not being able to have children of her own. She naturally felt my pregnancy was unspeakably sinful and unfair.

Louise was to be entrusted to my care for only a few hours, but when Friday came around and Ann left for her funeral, I was petrified. 'You'll be *fine*,' Mary reassured me. 'It's all instinctive.' But it was scant reassurance, because when I told her I'd never held a baby before, she looked at me incredulously. 'What — *never?*'

It seemed incredible to me too, once I gave it some thought, but it was true, and as I went into the nursery to give Louise the first of her two feeds, I felt wholly inadequate for the task.

I picked her up – she was crying, of course; they all either slept or cried – and gingerly eased my hand under her tiny skull. This seemed to calm her immediately, which helped my confidence a lot, but then she started to cry again. It wasn't her mother picking her up, and I sensed she knew that. As I lowered us both onto the nursing chair beside the cot, I felt the weight of the world in the shape of this tiny little human. Where would she end up? What would her future be like when she left the convent? How could Ann, now she'd given birth to her, bear to part with her?

Tentatively I pushed the teat of the bottle into her tiny open mouth, and almost immediately the crying stopped and was replaced by urgent sucking. She seemed so strong, her little lips really tugging on the bottle. As she fed, her expression became dreamy and faraway, softening her angry features as if by magic.

I was all at sea again once the bottle was empty. Louise had fallen into what looked like a deep and dreamy slumber, but I would have to wake her up to change her nappy. She protested loudly as I got up and took her over to the changing mat, and even more as I tried gently to remove her clothes. How horrible it must be, I thought, to be a baby in this place. It was so cheerless and cold – all hard surfaces and draughts. I knew I was making things worse with my ineptitude. The nappies were so big. There was so much cloth, so many corners, so much stiff, scratchy towelling – and I had so little sense of what to do with it. All the while Louise was looking up at me, fractious and bewildered and uncomfortable, as the chill air of the cavernous nursery began to turn her little legs blue.

'Here, let me help,' said one of the other mothers, who'd joined me at the counter. I'd been taking so long over everything, she was the only other girl left in the nursery. 'It's almost too painful to watch you!' she said, smiling warmly. Once again, I could only stand and marvel as she showed me the correct way to fold the nappy, how to lay it beneath the baby and how to deal with both the fabric and the scary nappy pins.

'There,' she said proudly, before returning to her own baby. 'That'll give you a head start when your own little one comes along.'

She looked about eighteen, and could have been even younger, but she seemed so efficient, so calm, so untroubled by her baby's angry kicking. 'How old is he?' I asked her, as she re-dressed her little boy. 'Close on six weeks now,' she said. 'He's just gorgeous, isn't he?'

I agreed that he was, as she picked him up again. She held him to her face, just as Ann had done. It was almost like she was trying to drink in the scent of him. 'Not long now,' she said, giving me a wry half-smile. 'Less than two weeks.' She kissed him again. 'It's all gone too fast – much too fast.'

The light caught her face and despite her cheerful demeanour I could see tears shining in her eyes. 'How can you bear it?' I asked, because I genuinely wanted to know. I just couldn't see myself there, having to *be* her, having to be so brave.

'I don't know,' she said. 'I'm not even sure I can yet. But I'm going to have to bear it, aren't I? What else is to be done?'

As she relinquished her baby to the jaws of his cot and hur-ried from the nursery to resume her chores, I wished I knew her story. Where had she come from? What was she going back to when she left? But then, I thought, I already knew her story, didn't I? It was the same as mine – wretched. And she was right: there was nothing to be done about it.

What a horrible, unfeeling world we both lived in, I thought, as I picked Louise up to return her to her cot. She was wide awake now, and once again crying loudly, and I hated the thought of having to dump her onto the hard, unyielding mattress, knowing she'd have to cry herself to sleep. To make matters worse, just at the moment when I was about to lay her down, she was violently sick, vomiting up what looked like half the bottle's worth of baby milk in one great rush of liquid that spewed all down her front.

Having ejected the milk, she immediately looked happier, but she was now soaking. The front of her nightie was drenched. I'd have to change it. I couldn't leave her like that. She'd get hungry again, and there was nothing I could do about that, but she'd also get chilled to the bone lying in wet clothing. I carefully placed her in her cot and went to look in her locker; Ann had shown me where I could find a change of clothing.

I knew that I had to be quick, but I wasn't quick enough. I'd just gathered up Louise and a dry nightie when I heard Sister Teresa's voice rasping behind me.

'Angela!' she snapped. 'There you are! Why are you still in here? Why aren't you attending to your duties?'

I felt a rush of defiance flood my cheeks. She knew full well that I'd agreed to look after Ann's baby, so where did she think I was?

'I'm changing Louise,' I explained. 'She's—'

'*Still*?' she interrupted, looking genuinely incredulous. 'You've been in here for ages. What on earth have you been doing all this time? Is she fed?'

'Yes, she's fed.'

'And have you changed her yet?' She looked from me to the baby.

I nodded. 'Yes, yes, I've changed her nappy, but—'

'So why are you still here? Put her back in her cot, for pity's sake!' She glanced around her. 'All this noise! You're disturbing the other babies!'

Not as much, I thought crossly, as you are. I kept my own voice pointedly low. 'It's just that she's been sick all down her front,' I persisted. 'I wanted to put her in a dry nightie, so that—'

'For goodness' *sake*!' Sister Teresa barked, marching towards me now. 'Fuss, fuss, fuss. Give her to me . . .' She held her hands out and irritably flapped her bony fingers towards me. 'Come on,' she said, taking Louise from me. I thought for a moment that she was going to change Louise for me, but I was instantly disabused of such a fanciful notion. 'Now put that nightie back where you found it and get back to the milk kitchen. There's work to be done. For goodness' sake,' she rasped, heading back to Louise's place in the line, 'a little posset down her front isn't going to *kill* her, Angela!' Then, as I watched, she deposited the now howling baby on the mattress. 'Go on,' she said, turning, and making shooing motions in my direction. 'Why are you still here? There's work that needs to be done. Get back to your duties.'

As I made my way back to the milk kitchen, feeling I'd let Ann down badly, I couldn't help but be incredulous. This was a *nun*. Someone I'd been taught was a person with a vocation to do God's work on earth – wasn't that the idea? If Sister Teresa was supposed to typify such a person, then the world had gone mad, I decided.

It was a world that, for me, had seen major upheavals. My father's death had brought about many changes in our family, not least of which was that my mother, always the disciplinarian, became doubly strict, feeling the need to take on the roles of both mother *and* father. My whereabouts and my companions had to be known to her at all times. Boyfriends were vetted – embarrassingly. Whenever they called for me, she would confront them on the doorstep, explaining that she was my voice for the present and I was most definitely unavailable. It wasn't surprising that hardly any boys passed muster, as she reasoned that my father would never have approved of them.

Some relief from this maternal pressure came with the arrival of my stepfather, Sam, into our lives in the summer of 1961. My mother had been introduced to him by a family friend and they'd soon struck up a friendship.

When I first met my future stepfather, I'd immediately felt apprehensive. He was a 53-year-old bachelor who had lived with his mother until her death a couple of years earlier. What on earth did he know of family life? His values were frankly Victorian. It was clear that he took a lofty moral stance in all things, and had a pretty dim view of what he perceived as a laxity in the way I was disciplined. I was, as he and my mother kept repeating, his concern now too, at least until I reached the age of twenty-one.

It was a decidedly quick courtship. They were married in March of 1962, and we all moved into his bungalow in another part of Essex. My mother was given free rein to transform his home – now also ours – and enjoyed freedom from constant financial anxiety. There was more freedom for me too. Though providing something else for my mother to focus on besides me, the move to Sam's bungalow created logistical problems, as it was miles away from where we'd lived before. But I didn't mind. I was eighteen – almost an adult. My friends now being somewhat distant geographically, I could at last enjoy some respite from questions and curfews, as whenever we socialised together, it was much more practical for me to stay overnight with them. Just as my mother relished having a man in her life, I relished her being less present in mine.

It seemed a guardian angel was looking out for me professionally as well. Since my father's death and the end of my educational aspirations, I'd resigned myself to not having any sort of career; I fully expected that I would see out my days in the typing pool of some large conglomerate. Quite by chance, however, a neighbour approached my mother and asked her when I would be leaving secretarial college. It seemed her sister was retiring from her job very shortly, and was on the lookout for a new young replacement to train.

The woman was a codes translator in a large City of London firm of importers and exporters called Guthrie and Co. It was a job that involved making sense of and compiling instructions in the vast array of complex codes that were used as a means of secure communication in the global shipping industry. And so it was that I was given the chance of a lifetime, and began what would turn out to be some of the happiest years of my life. I worked with two wonderful women, who remain lifelong friends; I had a wise and warm boss, who taught me so many new skills, and I couldn't quite believe my good fortune. To be earning good money doing something I loved so much was icing on an already delicious cake.

Yes, I was an innocent, but emerging into adulthood at the start of the 1960s, it seemed that the possibilities were endless. I had embarked on a career, I had my whole life ahead of me and I was determined that one day I would look like the glamorous and sophisticated women that I passed on the City streets each day.

But look at me now, I thought, as I finished my second milk round and headed to the dining room for tea that afternoon. I still felt terrible about poor Louise, who'd been so cold and wet and ravenous when I'd done her second feed. I looked around for Ann, but it seemed she hadn't returned yet; instead it was the usual sea of hollow-eyed girls. There were no sophisticated followers of fashion round the dining table in the Loreto Convent Mother and Baby Home, for sure – just a group of desperate young women who were paying the painful price of what, in every single case I heard, was not so much sinful as tragic, however much the nuns kept telling us otherwise.

'So what's your story?' asked Linda, as we took our places at the table. Linda was one of the girls I'd recently befriended, who'd arrived at the convent the previous week. She was from Bradford, and was a ray of sunshine in the gloom, with a relentlessly positive and infectious personality.

Our different duties were very isolating, as we tended to perform them alone, so I was glad of the chance to sit down and have a proper chat with her. I told her the bare bones of what had happened with Peter.

'Bastard,' was her considered reply.

'And you?' I asked, expecting something less terrible, somehow. That was silly though. She was here as well, wasn't she?

'Another bastard,' she said. Then she leaned in towards me. 'In fact, on balance, an even bigger one.'

'What happened?'

'What's happened is that he's married,' she said.

'I'm so sorry,' I began. This was a depressingly common story.

'Trust me, not half as sorry as I am,' she finished. 'I only found out two days ago!'

I was shocked, and said so.

'Me too,' she went on. 'Me too! I had no idea – not even an inkling. But, of course, now everything's falling into place. I mean, I'm nineteen, he's not much older, and we weren't ready for marriage, or so *I* thought, so when he wanted me to have an abortion – and let me tell you, he *really* wanted me to have an abortion – it didn't seem like anything unusual. I wasn't going to have one, though. No way. I mean, you hear the stories, don't you?' She shuddered and pulled a face. 'So I got everything organised, so I could, you know, get down here and have the baby. Got a job in London, so my mam wouldn't find out anything about it. Jesus! The lies I tell her, God save my soul . . .'

'So what happened?' I asked her. 'How did you find out he was married?'

'When I called him on Wednesday,' she told me. 'Just this last Wednesday! Can you believe it? Anyway, you know, I called him just to have a chat, as you do. We've been speaking on the phone regularly. All the time, you know? All the way through this. And I thought – well, as you do – that however horrible this is, at least I had him to support me, to go back to. At least we could pick up

where we left off, you know? But when I called on Wednesday . . . '
I could sense the tone of her voice changing. 'This woman
answered, because he wasn't there; he was out of the office or
something. And she was like, "Oh, is that his wife?"'

'Oh, that's awful!' I said, reaching instinctively to put an arm
around her. But she flapped her hand.

'Don't,' she said. 'Please don't. No sympathy allowed. I'm
okay so long as no one tries to give me a hug or anything. I'll be
okay . . .' She gave me a wobbly smile. 'I'm fine now. I'll get over
it. No bloody choice, have I? So,' she said, picking up her cutlery
with a clatter, 'this looks delicious, doesn't it?' And she began
eating.

Linda wasn't the only one who'd found out the hard way how
unjust life could be. The other girl I'd befriended, a lovely eighteen year old from Cromer called Pauline, had also got pregnant
by a long-term boyfriend, whom she'd loved, a young Italian boy
called Alessandro. He was another student at the college where
she was studying.

Sadly, but also depressingly common, as soon as Pauline had
told him she was pregnant, he wanted nothing more to do with
her. He was only seventeen and he was terrified, she told me. His
family back in Italy would have been horrified, plus he couldn't
face the prospect of being tied down with a baby at such a young
age.

And it was really that easy – for most of the boys, anyway.
They could just walk away, disappear, wash their hands of the
whole thing. It seemed desperately, horribly unfair.

In some ways my situation was simpler than most girls'. My mother knew what had happened, which meant I didn't have to lie to her. I also had a good job I'd been promised I could return to after the adoption and friends who would be there to support me. I was grateful that there weren't complications with the baby's father, as he had long since been out of the picture, happily oblivious to the consequence of our one night of folly. At least I didn't have to deal with a broken heart on top of everything else.

But in that respect I was painfully naive. I would soon experience true heartbreak.

Chapter Six

On 16 October I celebrated my twentieth birthday. The day was marked, as birthdays are, by a number of cards: one from my mother and stepfather, two more from my brothers and their families, plus a selection from those good friends and colleagues from Guthrie's who knew that my extended sojourn in sunny Italy was a fabrication.

I also received cards from Linda, Pauline and Mary, though the day itself was much like any other. The nuns were quick to discourage anything that might feel too 'fun', as being at odds with the tone of life in the convent and inappropriate, given the gravity of our situation and our need to pay penance for our sins.

This birthday was something of a watershed: not quite the customary watershed of reaching the magic number twenty-one, with its freedoms and responsibilities, but one that nevertheless marked the end of my teens and being on the cusp of becoming a grown-up. Except I felt I'd already grown up too much, and another birthday was approaching that was so much more important than mine. It was now playing on my mind almost constantly. I knew the birth of my baby would mean much more than a new anniversary to go into the calendar; it would haunt me for ever.

Angela Patrick

As the days following my birthday took me closer to my baby's, things were getting more and more difficult physically. I already had some experience of this, albeit vicariously, as I'd seen several of the girls go into premature labour. The accepted view was that it was often caused by the gruelling work schedule and the sheer brute physicality of what we had to do each day. No lying around and resting with your feet up was allowed in Loreto Convent. Just as the elderly nuns worked their fingers to the bone, we girls were given no quarter for being heavily pregnant. Indeed, if anyone dared stop to rest their legs, they would be treated not only with disdain but with nastiness too.

'Look at her, with her airs and graces!' the nuns would say to each other, always within earshot. 'What does she think this place is? A hotel?'

As a girl from a convent school, I should have been used to it. But I never did get used to it. How could I? It seemed to me to be so unnecessarily unpleasant, and so at odds with the accepted idea of what giving your life to God – what being a nun – meant. Nuns were supposed to personify goodness. Wasn't that how it was meant to be? So how could nuns – the living embodiment of kindness and selflessness – behave like such catty playground bullies?

They seemed to delight in belittling us and scolding us, as if we were lesser human beings because we had not taken the same lofty path they had. So they worked us accordingly. We were expected to carry on with our duties as normal until the very point we went into labour. More than once I remember privately giving thanks for my assigned job; yes, it was lonely and involved being on my feet for long periods, but it was nothing compared to manning the huge laundry vats, or endlessly scrubbing already scrubbed floors on your knees. For all of us the punishing schedule felt like a form of atonement in itself. It seemed designed to ensure that every part of our experience of labour and motherhood etched indelible negative memories on our brains, so we would never do anything as wicked again.

Births took place at St Margaret's Hospital in Epping, three miles away, and our final antenatal appointments were scheduled to take place there, normally for a week or so before our due dates. As ever, we would travel to our appointments alone on the bus, most of us wearing our 'wedding' rings.

Though things were becoming uncomfortable for me as the expected date loomed, I was showing no sign of going into labour any time soon. So when I arrived at my last scheduled antenatal appointment, the doctor examined me and told me to prepare to be induced.

'Not much happening in there, by the looks of things,' he told me. 'So ... let me see ...' he consulted a calendar on the wall. 'If you haven't had your baby by the tenth of November, we'll induce you on ... let me see ... November twenty-fourth.'

I sat there and nodded my understanding as he said this but I didn't know what he was talking about. If I'd known almost nothing about babies and childbirth before my pregnancy, I still knew precious little even at this advanced stage, since my experience of pregnancy had been mostly one of covering up and pretending not to be. How could I have got any information? I'd had no opportunities to discuss things with other mothers. And

I couldn't ask my mother – who could have helped me so much – because, from the outset, she'd found it easier to avoid the subject at all costs. It was no wonder I'd arrived at the convent clueless.

Since then, what little else I had picked up in the way of facts was of questionable use. Yes, I was developing some understanding of the process, but in such miserable circumstances it was no surprise that all it did was scare me witless. It didn't help that when the girls returned from giving birth they invariably told stories of how horrible the nurses at the hospital had been to them.

Apart from other girls' horror stories, which I could hardly bring myself to listen to, no one in the convent told us anything. Where the nuns could, and perhaps should, have given us some advice on what might happen during labour, it was as if our situation was so shameful that it mustn't be spoken of, let alone voluntarily brought up and discussed. All I was told, once my due date came and went, and the 24th loomed ever closer, was that I must pack a bag and telephone my mother to let her know what was going on. If nothing had happened by the 24th, then I'd be admitted to hospital and my labour would be induced.

I duly phoned my mother, and it was as awkward a call as I'd known it would be. She sounded concerned, but she also seemed a lot more confident than I felt. It would be fine was all she kept saying. The nuns would look after me. And I really think she believed that, too. No wonder she felt calm: they would be taking good care of me. After all, why wouldn't she think that? She was a devout Catholic and, along with devout Catholics everywhere, she knew that nuns represented all that was good: comfort and care in times of need. And, to her mind, they were experienced at looking after errant young mothers and their unfortunate offspring. My mother thought I was in the hands of professionals. And she certainly had no words of advice for me about the birth. She didn't proffer any and I wouldn't have asked her; it wasn't the sort of thing we'd discuss.

Generally, when girls went into labour, an ambulance was called to take them to hospital, but this would not be the case for me.

'Right, Angela,' Sister Teresa had told me the day before, bustling into the dining room at teatime with a file. 'Your induction. If you don't go into labour overnight, then you'll have to go to hospital on the bus. I've checked the timetable and there's one that should get you there in ample time . . .'

'The *bus*?' I had mostly been too scared to speak out since our telling-off in the common room, but I was so shocked the words just popped out.

'Yes, the bus,' she snapped. 'How on earth else do you think you're going to get there? They don't just send ambulances willy-nilly, you know. And we certainly can't be expected to use valuable funds on fripperies such as taxis, if that was what you were thinking, young lady.'

I was stunned. I was almost forty-two weeks pregnant now. Huge. And what if something happened *on* the bus? What if my waters broke? I didn't know much about anything to do with childbirth, but I'd been told about this particular aspect, in excruciating detail, only last week. Horrible scenarios began queuing for attention. Surely they couldn't expect me to go all the way there by bus? It had been exhausting enough three weeks ago at my last antenatal appointment. This was inhuman, surely?

Sister Teresa must have read my mind. 'You know, Angela,' she sniffed at me, 'women all over the world give birth in the most difficult and appallingly unsanitary conditions every minute of every day, and you girls – *all* of you girls' – she cast an eye around now, knowing full well that everyone else would be listening – 'would do very well to remember that, and feel grateful that you have the support you do.' She flipped her file closed. 'So. Any questions? It leaves at 11.15 sharp.'

And with that she swooshed out and closed the dining-room door behind her.

'Don't panic,' said Pauline. 'It'll happen. I know it will. Come on, girls. Who wants to take bets on Angela going into labour tonight? Or, I know, perhaps we could do a rain dance or something!'

There was a ripple of laughter, but it was feeble. Everyone was subdued now, and too busy cradling their own bumps. I could only hope Pauline was right.

I lay awake till the small hours, trying to will my body into action, but when I woke up the next morning nothing had changed and I knew I would be making that journey to be induced as planned. How I envied Mary, who'd had her baby, Anthony, and been re-billeted in the mothers' dormitory. I missed her. She had made it through the ordeal that still lay ahead for me, and I would have so loved to hear some words of reassurance from her.

Eleven o'clock the following day saw me donning both my coat and a wedding ring – borrowed, this time, since my own was now too small to fit over my swollen finger – and walking alone to the bus stop with my overnight bag. It was like I was walking to my doom, waddling to the bus stop that Sunday morning. I was thankful that soon I would no longer feel like a whale, but it was scant compensation for everything else I was feeling.

I was so scared; the sense of abandonment was overwhelming. It was all I could do to stop big tears of self-pity from spilling out and plopping down my front. Where was my mother right now? What was *she* doing? Was she thinking about me, as I stood shivering and frightened at the bus stop? Did she even care? That no one else cared could not have been made clearer.

One thing I could rely on was that the nurses would treat me as a pariah. Everyone had said so. We were considered to be the lowest of the low. Would they be nasty to me? Shout and make me cry?

After a worrying journey, I was admitted to hospital at around 1.30 in the afternoon. I had some blood taken and filled in a long consent form, before I was taken to the maternity department to be induced. Hardly anyone spoke to me or proffered a reassuring smile. It was just go here, sign this, do that, sit down there, as if I were a package being processed.

My mind was racing by now, wondering what 'induced' might mean in practice. Would it be an injection? A pill? Some invasive kind of internal procedure? I badly wanted to know but I didn't dare make a nuisance of myself by asking, as it seemed the girls had been right: I was here on sufferance, and lucky to be considered human. And it seemed no one felt inclined to tell me anything, either.

I was finally shown into a tiny room with nothing other than a bed in the middle of it.

'There you are,' said the nurse, pointing to a starched hospital gown that was folded at the end of the thin mattress. 'Change into that, please. Everything off. I'll be back to you shortly. Okay?'

I did as she asked, feeling self-conscious about having the back flapping open, but I couldn't reach to do up the ties. I then sat heavily on the bed, my feet throbbing by now, and waited, listening to intermittent sounds of anguish coming from adjacent rooms and corridors. I didn't know what to do with myself.

Ten minutes later, the nurse was back, this time with a drip stand and kidney bowl. She put the latter on the bed beside me. 'Right,' she said, pulling a swab and some sort of syringe from it. 'I'm going to fix a drip in your arm now. It will be something like an hour or so before it takes effect, and then you'll start having contractions.'

She went then, the job done. She left me alone in the small room, watching the bubbles rise in little streams up the drip bag. The minutes ticked and ticked and ticked by, but nobody came, and I could feel the panic, like the bubbles, rise up inside me. Was it right for me to have to go through this all on my own? Was this what God wanted? To punish me like this? What sort of God would be so cruel?

I thought of Peter and how lightly God had let him off. Yes, it had been my choice not to tell him I was pregnant, but even if

I had done, what difference would that have made? Perhaps he would have offered money for an abortion, like Linda's boyfriend had. Perhaps he would have promised solidarity, expressing sympathy for my plight, or perhaps he would have run away, as Pauline's Alessandro had done. I had no way of knowing. One thing was for sure, though: it was me who had to do this now – alone.

Still, I wondered, having nothing else to do or fix my mind on, what was *he* doing now? Having fun somewhere, I didn't doubt, oblivious to the chain of events he'd set in motion, *we'd* set in motion. Why had I let him persuade me that he'd make it safe? Why had I been so gullible and naive?

When the first contraction came, it was like a rolling wave of discomfort that swept over my stomach like an arm sweeps across a radar display. Yes, it was more intense than the sensations I'd already been feeling, but not *so* different – not unmanageable, not too bad. I can do this, I thought. It will be okay. I *can* do this. If I could keep telling myself that, I'd be okay.

The hour had passed, but no one had come to see me. So I just lay there, on the bed, waiting for the next wave to roll in, trying to imagine myself lying on a beach, or in the sea, or in a meadow. Who'd suggested that? Was it Mary or one of the others? It didn't matter, so long as I was anywhere else.

Except I couldn't escape, because every time the waves rolled along, they took me to where *they* wanted me. And with each wave came the realisation that the pain was growing stronger and more scary. Very soon it was like being punched, but in slow motion. It made my teeth gnash and my toes curl involuntarily.

It was pain like no other I'd experienced – as if my torso had been taken over by creatures from outer space.

And then I heard a voice. 'Oh, you've started then,' it said crisply. 'That's good.' I opened my eyes. It was a different nurse. Her voice was kindly, even if she didn't have much to say – simply 'Right, let's check your pulse, then' and 'Just going to hook you up to the monitor', before disappearing out of the door once again.

The monitor being strapped to me was a welcome distraction. At least I had company of a sort now, as I could hear my baby's heartbeat: *p-tm, p-tm, p-tm* it went, so fast and so furious. Every time a new contraction came surging in towards me, the *p-tm, p-tm* sound would speed up even more. I could visualise my tiny baby being pummelled mercilessly by my muscles. *We'll get through this together*, I silently promised. *We will*.

There was a clock on the wall, a big white one. But time had seeped away; it had lost all sense, all meaning. I could only measure it in heartbeats and the spaces between them, the relationship between the pulsing and pounding in my temple and the beating of my baby's tiny heart, and the way the beats, and the timbre of the sound, rose and fell. With each rise, the pain – the biting twisting *agony* – of the contractions was building and building and building and building, each one more overwhelming and terrifying than the one before it. *P-tm, p-tm, p-tm, p-tm, p-tm* . . .

Where had the spaces between the pains gone? The contractions were coming relentlessly now, leaving me no space in which to breathe. Tears were falling from me, streaming out, a pair of hot tramlines that etched twin paths from the corners of my eyes to fill my ears. And still no one came, no one cared, no one helped me. Could God even see me here, wretched and writhing? Or had He too turned his back on me now?

Then another nurse appeared suddenly. Or was it the same one? I didn't know. Tall, brisk. Warm hands moved on my body, between my legs. I cried out then. 'How long now? I can't bear this! I can't *bear* this!' There was no response, no word of comfort, no connection, no reassurance. Just a blur of uniform, the metallic flash of wielded instruments, the crackle of a plastic apron, a hand on my thigh now, another on my distended belly. A sudden sharpness – like a knife's stab – seared through me, then a flood of warmth gushed between my thighs.

'A while,' she said. 'A while yet.' A while yet. A *while* yet? But how long must I suffer? How many heartbeats of agony? How much must I bear till I'd paid the price for my sin – my terrible, mortal sin. But I *was* mortal, wasn't I? How could God be so godless, so heartless, so cruel, so immune to my pleading and my pain?

My baby. I must try to think straight for my baby. I would bear it. I *could* bear it. I had to bear it, for it was coming – my child was *coming* – whether it wanted to be born into such wretchedness or not, it was coming; it was about to be born.

It grew dark as I writhed there, sopping and screaming. It grew darker. People came; people went. People raised their voices, and lowered their voices, forming a babble of white noise. I couldn't seem to grasp what was happening to me any more. I had lost all reason. I just drifted. I bobbed and sank with it. Oblivious.

Only the pain mattered, each new tsunami of agony coming faster than the one before it. I had no time to inhale, no time to cry. Then no breath to cry, only grunts, until I could no longer focus on anything outside of me. I had a desperate need to push, to expel, to keep pushing, to push this thing – this *massive* thing – out of my body. More noise. Was someone shouting? The head. Was it the head coming? Sudden lucidity: it *was* the head – oh my *GOD*. An unstoppable force built in me – a need to extrude, to force it from me, to get it out, to make it gone – but *HOW*?

I was pushing against something stronger than I was – God again, to make sure that I learned? That I atoned? That I could be in no doubt how much my wickedness would be repaid ten times over? It was etched in the faces that now swam before me. I was wicked. I had sinned. I must be punished. I must suffer. I must not seek help or solace. I had no right to expect it. I had sinned. I must expect and bear the consequences, the exquisitely perfect agony of feeling my body fight the very thing it had created.

Push, I chanted. Over and over and over. *Push. PUSH! Grit your teeth and push some more. Ignore the pain now, ignore the burning, ignore the fire – the fires of hell? Ignore the flames, ignore the fire. Just pay your price, just pay your price, just pay your price . . .*

And then a voice again. Incongruous. Exclamatory. 'Big shoulders!' *Big shoulders*, I heard someone say. *This baby has big shoulders*! This baby. *My* baby. My baby born of mortal sin.

'8.30,' the midwife said. 'It's a boy.'

*

I cried then. I sobbed and sobbed, as I held him, this tiny piece of me, in my arms. I was shaking by now, shivering, soaked with sweat. My legs clattering together like marionette limbs, uncontrollable, jerking on strings.

His hair – oh, his hair! Such a mop of black hair! Slick with blood, wet and coiling, atop his squashed angry face.

'Shhh,' I soothed as he railed at me, furiously alive now. 'Shhh,' as the nurses moved around me, a blur of blue cotton and metal instruments. *Shhh, baby, shhh. I'm here. Everything's okay.* But I soothed through fresh tears, as the love welled within me. It would *not* be okay. I had sinned, I had atoned, but it could never be okay. I had not paid my price yet. The pain of birth, of being ripped raw and torn – the excruciating, searing, stinging agony – was as nothing compared to what was to follow. I would be paying the price forever; this was only the beginning. The clock on the wall had already started counting down.

New mothers from Loreto Convent would normally be returned to the mother and baby home straight away – no stay in hospital, no visitors, no flowers. There would be no lingering, in their shame, to clutter up the place with a bad atmosphere. They would be sent straight back, with their babies, even as the blood dried and crusted around their stitches. They would then spend the first few days with their babies in the lying-in room at the convent, well away from the gaze of the society that so shunned them. But not me and my baby, apparently: it was ten at night and we must stay here.

'But why?' I asked, shocked, already anticipating and looking forward to my departure. I was desperate to go now, anxious to get away with my baby. I'd had so many stitches, each one more agonising than the last. It felt like my baby had been ripped out of me.

'For observation,' the midwife said, her voice clipped, her expression weary. 'You had a difficult delivery. The doctor wants to keep an eye on you.' She made a note on a clipboard attached to my bed. 'Someone will be along shortly to transfer you to the ward.'

I lay back against the pillow, anticipating another bout of waiting. My little boy was now serenely asleep. I was exhausted but couldn't close my eyes in my need to gaze at him. That he'd come from inside me and was now here nestled with me felt like the most incredible thing I had ever achieved in my life. But someone – a porter – did come only a few minutes later, and pushed me, and him, in my hospital bed to a dimly lit four-bedded ward.

As soon as I got there I realised that being parked in a corridor would have been infinitely preferable to the sight that greeted me. The minute I entered the ward, my hope – that my fellow occupants would be sleeping – was dashed. They were all very much awake and smiling at me, so I smiled wanly back. I felt small and scrutinised, and as though I'd been found wanting. Nothing could have highlighted the difference between us quite as effectively as the huge arrays of flowers and cards that seemed to fill every space that wasn't already occupied with beaming family members, now leaving, chatting excitedly and cooing over the tiny charges in their white metal cots.

The other mothers were all older than me, and looked almost alien; they seemed so happy, so assured, so full of life and love and laughter, whereas I, in contrast, was exhausted and tearful and frightened. It was as if on entering the ward I'd physically shrunk. How long would it be before they worked out that I wasn't one of them?

Not long. I had hoped I could roll on my side and sleep would claim me. But it wasn't to be. 'Was your husband with you at the birth?' the woman opposite me wanted to know, almost the minute the last visitor had left the ward. They were obviously curious to find out about me – this young girl who'd arrived without so much as a card or a bunch of flowers, let alone the baby's father or a single visitor.

I shook my head, my mind already automatically filling up with potential stories. I was used to this now, this lying on the hoof. I hated it so much. But what else could I do? Then it came to me. 'He's in South Africa,' I said, while inside my brain whirred frantically. 'He's working out there, temporarily . . .'

'Oh, I see,' the woman nodded, looking like she didn't.

'And he couldn't get back in time,' I explained. 'But he'll be home by the end of this week.'

'Oh, I see,' she said again. 'That's a shame.'

'Such a shame,' agreed the mother beside her. 'And what about your mother?'

'In Ireland,' I answered, turning over in bed painfully and wishing desperately to be left alone. My mother might just as well have been in Ireland, I thought wretchedly. How could she have let me go through what I'd just been through all alone? Why was no one here to care for me, love me, tell me how brave I'd been, or coo over and hug my perfect baby?

I knew they didn't believe me. And they probably knew I knew it, too. It was just a ridiculous façade we all had to maintain because the truth was so difficult to swallow. There I was, alone, my locker top empty apart from a big jug of water, and my two visitors' chairs depressingly vacant, on what by anyone's yardstick was *the* day for loving families, for the celebration of a new life joining them.

I must have fallen asleep after they took my baby over to the nursery for the night, because the next thing I remember was being woken. It was dawn, and, once I'd been examined and my stitches humiliatingly peered at, I was informed I could leave soon. And I was thankful. Unbelievable as it would have seemed to me before this, I was desperate to get back to the anonymity and sanctuary of the mother and baby home, away from the shame and embarrassment. I hated everyone's scrutiny, conscious that my ineptitude as I fed and clumsily changed my little boy would make it so obvious that I'd lied, that I wasn't one of them.

I was also in a great deal of pain. It felt like my insides had been ripped to shreds, my lower body rent asunder. Every step, every movement caused daggers of burning pain. If the nuns who had sent me here were from an Order of Divine Motherhood, the likes of me – their luckless charges – were from a place far below. There was nothing divine about my experience of motherhood so far.

I dressed myself in agony, and dressed my tiny infant in Emmie's thoughtfully knitted little baby clothes in agony, before making a torturous, shuffling exit from the ward to a waiting ambulance and falling into a stupor for the journey home, despite a non-stop commentary of inane comments from the driver.

It was only once I had made the excruciating journey up a flight of stairs and was installed in the bed in the lying-in room that I began to take proper conscious stock of my baby, my immediate surroundings and my new life. I was no longer billeted in the little room I'd been staying in, and my possessions had already been transferred here – one of the nuns had probably had one of the girls do it first thing this morning, I imagined. The move from one room to another seemed to be a metaphor for what had just happened to me, for the twenty-four hours that had completely changed my life. I had left the convent this time yesterday a naive young girl, pregnant, unmarried and in a state of mortal sin, and had returned today – albeit, in the eyes of my church, the same sinful young woman – another person, different in every way. I had become a mother. I had given birth. I had had a baby.

I decided to call him Paul, because it was a name I'd always liked. I had chosen the name Paul for a boy very early in my pregnancy, and, ironically perhaps, Teresa for a girl. The latter had been abandoned when I'd arrived at the convent, for obvious reasons, and I'd switched my allegiance to Bernadette, but I hadn't had long to consider alternative girls' names.

As my baby lay there beside me, asleep and untroubled in his crib, for perhaps the first time since he'd been born, I studied Paul properly. His mop of hair, so very thick and dark, mesmerised me. As did his eyes – those questioning eyes newborn babies always seem to have – they were so blue against his skin, which was olive, just like mine. He'd got that colouring from the Spanish blood on my mother's side of the family. In fact, I could see so much of myself and my family in him that it took my breath away. He really was an extension of me. This was very much *my* baby.

He had an array of little sounds he'd make, peculiar just to him, and I wondered the same thing any new mother would when he made them: what did they mean? Was he hungry? Was he content? Was he sleepy? I also felt the same fears that any novice mother would: that my ignorance of how to care for him might distress him. Though, of course, Mary had been right: looking after your own newborn *is* instinctive, and in reality we were completely in tune.

I would look at him and marvel at everything I had gone through to get him – all the unhappiness and the guilt and the pain of giving birth – which now seemed unimportant, a world away, forgotten. But one fact was inescapable: the biggest ordeal was yet to come. Though my baby and I would be parted in a few weeks, there was no going back for me emotionally; I was Paul's mother and I would love him forever.

Chapter Seven

I felt the weight of the coming adoption pressing down on me like a death sentence during those first hours and days. I had given birth to my son knowing only too well that soon he would no longer be mine. Not surprisingly, then, I cherished our brief time in the lying-in room at Loreto Convent, perhaps even more than I might have done if I'd had the luxury of knowing a shared future stretched out ahead of us. I couldn't allow myself to entertain that prospect, even as I cradled this tiny piece of me in my arms.

I was happy to be cocooned from the outside world, which carried on without me. I would know nothing of the assassination of President Kennedy until a full week after it had happened – not until I was moved into the dormitory with the other mothers. It was as if time wanted to be kind to me, just for a little while, and stand still.

But there *was* something I did find out about – something shocking. That first evening, while Paul was sleeping, I made my way painfully downstairs to phone Emmie and John. I was so anxious to hear the sound of a loving voice, to talk to someone I knew would want to hear about my baby. It was Emmie who answered, and right away she seemed unexpectedly emotional.

'Oh, Angela!' she cried, when she realised who it was. 'I'm so, so glad to hear your voice! How *are* you?'

'Tired,' I said. 'In quite a lot of pain from my stitches, but otherwise I'm—'

'Oh, you poor, poor thing. Are you still in hospital? Because I was speaking to John, and he wasn't sure if they'd let you out yet—'

'No, no. They brought me back here this morning,' I told her. 'They only kept me in overnight.'

'Oh, that's such a relief. I did speak to your mother this morning and she told me the nuns had said you were doing okay, but, well, as you can imagine, I've been thinking about you every single *minute*. We were all so worried about you, and the baby, of course, and they hardly told us anything about what had been going on . . .'

'Worried about what?' I said, confused by both her words and her anxious tone. 'Who didn't tell you anything?'

'The hospital! I mean we drove all that way, and then—'

'Drove where? To the hospital? When was this?'

'When you were in labour yesterday, of course.' There was a pause. 'Didn't you know?'

I told her I didn't. I was reeling. Emmie had actually been at the hospital? How could I not have remembered that?

'I have no memory of that at *all*,' I told her. 'How can that be? I mean, I know I was in a lot of pain, but I hadn't been given any drugs or anything . . .'

'But you wouldn't,' she said. 'Because we didn't actually see you.'

I was very confused now. 'But why were you there anyway? You didn't know when I was going in, did you?'

'No,' she said. 'Not till your mum rang.'

'Mum rang?'

'Yes, she called John when the hospital called her. She needed to be driven there—'

'To the hospital? While I was in labour?'

'Yes. God, how did you not know this?'

'I knew nothing about it, Emmie. Nothing at all.'

'Well, you were in a pretty bad way, by all accounts. That's why they asked her to go there.'

'They were that worried?' I was finding this difficult to take in. 'I had no idea.'

'Apparently so. That's what your mum told us, anyway. So we picked her up and drove her there, but by the time we arrived they told us that everything was okay again. That the baby had been born and you were both safe and well.'

'And they wouldn't let you *see* me?'

'They said you were having stitches.' She paused again. 'And, well, to be honest, your mum felt . . . well, that maybe you would need to sleep after that, and . . . well, it was difficult for her, obviously. So we brought her home again.' She paused. 'Sweetheart, you know how it is . . .'

I did know how it was only too well. If my mother had come to see me, then everyone would *know* she was my mother. 'I know,' I said. 'But, even so, you would have thought, under the circumstances . . .'

'I know, sweetie, I know.' Emmie paused again. She probably

didn't know what to say to me. And I understood. What *could* she say? 'Anyway,' she went on finally. 'I've been keeping up to date – I don't have the number there, and I wasn't sure if I was allowed to call, which is why I'm so glad to hear from you . . . oh, it's *so* good to hear from you, I can't tell you, Angela. So, tell me all about your lovely boy. I've been *dying* to hear. What does he look like? Is he gorgeous? What have you called him?'

Going back to the lying-in room after speaking to Emmie, I wasn't sure what to feel. I had given birth only once – I had nothing with which to compare it – but to find out that the hospital had deemed it necessary to summon my mother, as next of kin, was a lot to take in. How bad *had* things been? No one had said a word to me about it – not a word. And I doubted anyone would now it was all over. Unless I demanded to see my medical records, I realised it was unlikely I'd ever know what had really happened.

Far more shocking was the realisation that my mother *had* been there at the hospital, only a couple of walls away from me perhaps. She had been there, and even then couldn't bring herself to come and see me, to check on me and reassure herself I was okay, to offer a crumb of comfort when I had so badly craved one. She'd been content to be told that all was well and then leave. I felt stunned, tearful, angry. How could shame be a more powerful emotion than maternal love?

Perhaps because of this – or maybe it would have happened anyway – I retreated into my own little world of maternal love instead. I would not have Paul for long, but for as long as I did have him I would love him and care for him with every fibre of my being. I wanted nothing more than to stay in my cocoon with him, because every thought of leaving it was accompanied by fear of a world that disapproved of me, judged me and wouldn't accept my right to motherhood, and of a future that wouldn't include my baby. The convent stopped feeling like a place of punishment or atonement, but instead became a place of safety, where my baby could be acknowledged and was cared for. As unlikely as it was, it had become a home.

It was so intense, that brief time we had together, my baby and I. It was a time in which the hours blurred into days almost without me noticing, a paradoxical mixture of intense emotion and love and the endurance of equally intense pain.

Because I'd had so many stitches, both internally and externally, even the simplest things, such as walking and sitting, were excruciatingly painful, and would be, I realised, for many days. I also had a new problem to contend with: my milk had come in, an agony that soon became equally excruciating. But the pain could not, under any circumstances, be alleviated as nature intended, because breastfeeding was strictly forbidden at the convent. I don't know if this was because the nuns had decided it would make the coming separation harder for both mother and baby or because it was the prevailing fashion of the day – at that time, formula milk was marketed as a form of liberation, and young mothers were taking to it in droves. Perhaps it was another form of atonement that was designed to punish the mother but also punished the baby. I still don't know. Like every other mother further up the line, I simply accepted that breastfeeding was not an option. It hurt to have a part of my body trying to do one thing, but being made to do another, despite the pills I was given to dry up my milk. In the meantime, I just had to endure it.

Despite all the pain and discomfort, not to mention my complete ignorance of how to hold him and what to do for him, my little son and I enjoyed moments of pure bliss. Sister Teresa had taken over my milk kitchen duties and I left the room only for meals during those first four days. I even received my mother and stepfather there when they came to see us on the second day.

That visit was incredibly difficult. It would have been naive of me, I suppose, to expect it to be any different, even if I hadn't known about her coming to the hospital. My mother was now coming to visit the daughter she'd felt she had no choice but to abandon to her fate all those months back; the daughter who was caring for a newborn grandchild that she would never see again.

'How are you, Angela?' she said stiffly as she entered.

'I'm fine,' I told her, following up her platitude with my own.

I had decided that I would only mention her visit to the hospital if she did, and I suspected she would not. And she didn't – not in words. Nevertheless, on that day, she did express real emotions about what had happened to me, emotions other than disappointment and anger at my folly and shame.

'May I see him?' she asked, gesturing towards the cot beyond the bed. So formal. So not like a grandmother.

I nodded, and she went around to peer in at my sleeping child.

'He's beautiful,' she said, her voice cracking as she spoke. Though I could only see her face in profile, I knew she was struggling not to cry.

It hit me then, hard: I really was going to have to give up my baby. Up until the moment my mother broke down on seeing her little grandson, I had nursed a hope – albeit one that was deeply buried and never, ever voiced – that she would have a change of heart about him being adopted and admit she was wrong about what was best for both of us; that somehow we'd find a way for me to keep him; that she'd support me and help me and the nightmare could end.

But it was clear to me, watching her sniffing and dabbing at her wet eyes with a hankie, that there was no change of heart now nor would there ever be. She didn't *want* to be his grandmother. It was a role that she'd relinquished. She was crying because the reality of things had hit home for her too. She was crying in anticipation of my loss.

My stepfather spoke little and was only a stiff, sombre presence in the corner that day. I think he had long ago settled into his position that none of this was anything to do with him – with either one of them, in fact.

When Paul was five days old Sister Teresa removed my stitches, snipping them and slipping them all out, one by one, as she did for all the new mothers. It was probably just as well that I couldn't see what she was doing, because she had very shaky fingers and extremely poor eyesight. I shut my eyes and tried not to visualise what was happening too much. I hated the thought of her seeing such an intimate part of me. And I suspect, given her calling, she found the task odious too.

This milestone marked the day when my safe little bubble burst and the sound of the ticking clock grew louder. Once my stitches had been removed and my wounds were declared healed, I was moved up to the big attic room to sleep with the other mothers.

Paul was baptised in the convent chapel by the visiting priest, and immediately afterwards transferred to the nursery full time. Affixed to the cot was a blue cardboard tag, one of a batch provided by Cow and Gate, who made the baby formula we used at the convent, and on it was written 'Paul Brown'; beneath that his birth weight was recorded: '8 lb 12 oz'.

My tiny son had been by my side, except for a part of the night, since I'd returned. Now we would begin the new daily routine that would see us through until the day we both left.

That first night, the first when I was up in the attic room while he was in the nursery, was incredibly difficult to bear. It was bad enough being separated from him for so long, but being able to hear him crying for me, specifically, amid the general cacophony – something I hadn't anticipated – made it nigh on impossible to sleep. All I wanted was to do what any mother would do: go to him, pick him up, comfort and cuddle him. I wished so hard that things could be different. But apart from what was necessary for feeding and changing, all contact with my baby was now forbidden.

At least I was back with the other girls again and could benefit from their empathy and support. The room for the mothers was a very large one on the top floor, which ran the length of the convent, with ceilings that sloped at either end. It resembled a soldiers' billet: a dozen beds, with a row of six down either side, each with its own bedside locker and a big empty space in between. The comparisons didn't end there. Given the diversity of occupants, some would be neat and tidy, others very messy, and the room would be inspected regularly by Sister Teresa or, occasionally, the Reverend Mother. Equally regularly, girls would be singled out and publicly berated for their slovenly ways and their generally poor characters.

'You dirty, dirty girl,' the Reverend Mother would snap at whoever was the object of her disgust that day. 'All airs and graces and la-di-da ways you might have, but you're no better than a common hussy!' The nastiness, the tone, the implication were all so clear. In our exhausted and emotional state, whichever of us had incurred her wrath would often be reduced to floods of tears. Again and again, it hit me: how could they be so cruel to us, these women of God? It sometimes seemed like sport to them.

The room was freezing; it was December now and ice would regularly form on the insides of the windows. Most of us, now decimated physically by the punishing routine, preferred to sleep in our clothes not just because of the cold but because there was such an early start after nights that were routinely wakeful. I would rise at 5.30, feed and change my poor hungry, screaming baby, wash and dress myself, and have my own breakfast. Then I'd make up all the bottles in the milk kitchen, do Paul's 10 a.m. feed, return to the milk kitchen and work until lunchtime, do Paul's 2 p.m. feed, then work again till 4, have an hour's break, eat supper and do the 6 p.m. feed. I would have some free time in the common room before the 10 p.m. feed, the last of the day, then I'd fall into bed, exhausted, around 11.

Sleep didn't come easily – how could it? – as I could always hear Paul's pitiful cries as I lay rigid in my bed. This would go on and on and on and was torture. My head was already filled with so many troubling images – his little hands turned almost blue by the cold in the nursery, the scary dents in his head made by the unforgiving cot bars – I could hardly bear the pain of knowing how distressed he must have been, and I slept very fitfully the whole time I was there.

There was no night feed, so the babies were starving after having to go so many hours between feeds. It would be unthinkable – bordering on child cruelty – today, but I couldn't go to him. None of us could go to our babies, unless the baby was very sick, in which case Sister Teresa would come for the mother. The nursery was completely out of bounds.

Even in the daytime the nursery was not a nice place, as the nuns were so zealous about us not doing anything for our babies beyond the bare minimum necessary for their survival. We were not allowed to interact lovingly with them, much less sit and play with them. If you so much as kissed a tiny head and were spotted doing so, the nuns would rebuke you, as I found out for myself when Paul was just two weeks old. I had already fed him and removed his sodden nappy. As he was awake and alert, I thought I'd give him a moment to kick his little legs a bit, free of that huge hunk of towelling. And as I did so, I tickled the dome of his tiny tummy, revelling in the feel of his perfectly smooth skin. Had I left it at that, perhaps no one would have noticed. But I stooped to kiss it just as Sister Roc was passing. I didn't know why she was there – she rarely went near the nursery, as it was Sister Teresa's territory – but she was in the doorway even so.

'What on *earth* do you think you're doing, Angela?' she wanted to know. She had made me jump and, colouring, I straightened up and snatched up his clean nappy. It felt as if I'd been caught kissing a boy behind the bike sheds. The distaste on her face certainly seemed to suggest I was overstepping the mark, as did her words. 'If you'd wanted to have a baby of your *own*,' she continued, 'you should have got married before having one, shouldn't you? Now hurry up and get that child dressed and back in his cot!'

'That child', 'baby of your *own*': it was remembering those words that convinced me the nuns forbade closeness not to spare us the anguish of bonding with and then losing our children; no, it seemed to me they forbade closeness because they felt we had no right. We had given birth to the babies, yes – *He's my baby!* I'd wanted to scream at her. *I created him!* – but we'd already relinquished them. We were simply a part of the production process, delivering up babies to people who *did* deserve them. What did God, I wonder, think about this cold, unfeeling place?

Perhaps it was a blessing that our babies were so exhausted all the time. In that state a bottle of warm milk acted almost like a drug. Our main struggle was to keep them awake long enough so that they finished their feeds, but at least asleep they gave the impression of contentment.

Despite everything – the tiredness, the cold and hunger, the dread of the future – that time with my baby was so special and so precious. I loved the tiny person in my care. As the bond between us grew, I treasured the moments we spent together. I loved that he instinctively knew I was his mother. How, if he was crying and then heard my voice, he would listen and stop, calming immediately as I picked him up and held him close to me. I couldn't imagine someone other than me taking care of him – it seemed too cruel, too unthinkable, too unbearable.

It was indicative of our increasingly gallows-type humour that the line of cots in the nursery was referred to as 'death row'. The business of moving up it, and taking your place at the head, was something I'd observed early on. In the dormitory we tried not to speak about it. Instead we worked hard at pretending the future didn't exist, messing about, as any group of girls in a dormitory would, and getting chastised by an irritable Reverend Mother. But for all the external lightness we had very heavy hearts. The thought of leaving was constantly on our minds, as other mothers and babies packed up their things and left and were never seen or heard of again. It was as if they had dropped off a cliff into an abyss, or had tumbled through some trapdoor into another world.

Thankfully, there were chinks of light in the gloom. John and Emmie came to visit. They would later admit to being horrified by what they saw – a heavily pregnant girl on her knees, scrubbing a doorstep, in a scene reminiscent of a Victorian workhouse – and to being terribly upset for me, but it gave me such a boost to see their warm, smiling faces and to receive the tuck box they'd prepared for me full of lovely goodies. Though it was a painful reminder of what lay just around the corner, I was touched at how hard Emmie had been toiling away for me, knitting another whole array of baby clothes for Paul – matinée jackets, booties and mittens, as well as a hat and shawl – so I would have some beautiful things in which to dress him.

Emmie and John weren't allowed to see Paul. Having been turned away once already at the hospital, they were again denied the chance to meet him at the convent. Though they had been able to spend an hour with me, and I'd been so sure they'd be able to see Paul in the nursery, it was made clear that this was not an option.

'I'm sorry,' the Reverend Mother said, when we approached her to ask. 'But we don't allow visitors into the nursery. It's too disruptive.'

'We'll be quiet as mice,' Emmie tried boldly, 'I promise. We just want to look at him. We won't wake him up.'

'It's not a question of waking the babies,' the Reverend Mother replied firmly. 'It's a question of propriety.'

I knew very well what she meant by propriety, even if she stopped short of spelling it out to Emmie. In the eyes of the nuns, these babies shouldn't be seen and cooed over by biological relatives, who mustn't be regarded as family; these babies didn't have their family yet. They were just, temporarily, in a kind of baby laundry, biding their time until all concerned could wash their hands of them.

A couple of weeks later, thankfully, Sister Teresa did relent in this regard, when my older brother Ray and his wife Jean came one Sunday afternoon. The visit had started badly, as they'd had the temerity to turn up without having first received permission from the Reverend Mother, but they'd travelled a long distance and my brother had been somewhat stunned, to put it mildly, to have come so far only to be told by a nun that they could see me but not my baby.

I had to beg and plead, but eventually Sister Teresa permitted them a short visit to the nursery to see him. We were escorted to the nursery door where, under Sister Teresa's beady eye, they were allowed to gaze upon my tiny sleeping infant – no touching, no holding, no cuddling, just a brief look – and, as was the way at Loreto, only from a distance.

Chapter Eight

On Boxing Day I was allowed out. Being permitted to escape the confines of the convent for more than a brief trip to the shops was probably only marginally less difficult than escaping from a high security prison. Although there were no physical barriers to prevent girls going out, such was the power of the nuns that no one dared put their authority to the test. In order to secure my day release, my brother John had to make an application for me to be granted permission by telephone, and then had to wait while the nuns gave it consideration.

On the whole, visits were discouraged, and would be granted only if the nuns couldn't find a reason not to allow them, as when Ann had been allowed to attend a family funeral. Since it was Christmas, however, my visit would be sanctioned if I could find a girl willing to attend to Paul's feeds during the few hours I would be away.

Though I knew my family – well, John and Emmie, certainly – were keen on me making the visit home, privately I had mixed emotions. Yes, I'd felt homesick on Christmas Day without family members around me, but now I had a new familial bond to consider. The one highlight of the day had been spending a small part of it with my baby. Now I felt terribly anxious about leaving him.

I was also all too aware, given the contact we'd had thus far, that I would be expected not to talk about Paul and, while I was there, to behave as if he didn't exist, as if none of what had happened to me had taken place. The reality, of course, was that he was my whole world and I was his; I was the only thing he *had* in the world.

Christmas Day had been relatively low key at the convent, though we were determined to celebrate our babies' first Christmases as best we could. We knew it would be our last Christmas with them. For a couple of the girls, it would also be their last precious days together.

I had been down to the village and bought Paul a couple of Christmas presents, withdrawing a little money from my Post Office account. I'd bought him a teething ring, and a little soft toy – a white fluffy dog that now sat at the bottom of his cot. I'd also given him a rosary from the Catholic Repository – every Catholic child was given one – which I intended would go with him once he was adopted.

A rosary is an important Catholic artefact and very personal; though I still have my mother's, they are often put in a person's coffin with them. I made a conscious decision to keep Paul's in the end – almost as if I was retaining a little piece of him. Whenever I said prayers on his rosary, those prayers would be for him and would bring us together, if not in body, at least in spirit.

For most of the girls, normal chores were suspended on

Christmas Day, but as my job in the milk kitchen still needed to be done, I dealt with all the bottles as usual. I didn't mind. My frequent visits to the nursery meant that even if I couldn't hold my dear baby while I was doing my duties, I could see him.

The nuns softened towards us slightly on Christmas morning. There was no Christmas tree, as it would have been considered superficial on a day that was supposed to be celebrating Christ's birth, but they provided crackers for our Christmas lunch of turkey and plum pudding, and they'd allowed us to make and put up some paper chains.

The trappings of Christmas didn't really matter. What mattered most was that we were lucky enough to share this Christmas with our babies – an accident of timing, but a precious one. It felt as if we were living in a cocoon, with the outside world, for this brief time, non-existent.

Boxing Day, in contrast, drew me back to the real world. John and Emmie arrived in John's maroon Ford Anglia at 11.00 in the morning to drive me to Sam's bungalow – my former home – where the family, including my childless Aunt Ellen and Uncle Jack, traditionally spent the day.

I had asked one of the pregnant girls to look after Paul. She was a shy teenager called Carol; she was keen to be helpful, and I'd given her a list of all the things she needed to know.

By now Paul and I had developed quite a routine together. Carol must give him half his feed first – that was important, as he'd always be screaming for his bottle when I got to him – wind him halfway through, then change his nappy. She must remember to put on a little zinc and castor oil cream, then give him the remainder of his feed, before swaddling him securely and laying him back in his cot on his side.

Despite knowing he could come to no harm in my absence, it was disturbing to be putting physical distance between us voluntarily. As I put my warm coat on and went into the hall to wait for Emmie and John's arrival, it felt as if I'd left a part of myself behind.

It was a bitterly cold day that had begun with a deep frost, which never really looked like it would thaw. As I stepped out to greet them, I could feel the icy air catch in my nostrils; it was such a contrast to the air within the convent walls. I realised I had barely ventured into the outside world since the birth.

'Goodness!' said Emmie, leaping out of the car and rushing up to hug me. 'You don't look at *all* as if you've just had a baby! I can't believe you got your figure back so quickly!' She let me go and led me back to the waiting car and my brother. 'Look at her, John,' she said as she opened the door for me. 'Already back in her normal clothes!'

'What I have of them,' I said, as I got into the warm car. 'That's one of the things I really have to do today: bring some more clothes back with me. But you're right. It's amazed me. My bump must have been all baby!' That, I reflected, plus a subsistence diet, a heavy physical work schedule, many, many sleepless nights and a great deal of appetite-suppressing heartache. But it was so nice to see my brother and sister-in-law that I didn't want to gripe. At least with them I could be myself. At least with them I didn't have to hang my head in shame.

'What time do you have to be back?' John asked, as we sped away.

'Nine o'clock,' I said. 'Sharp.'

My brother grinned at me through the rear-view mirror. It was so good to see him. 'Absolutely no problem,' he replied. 'Wouldn't want to be in Reverend Mother's bad books . . .'

It was strange to be speeding along the deserted country roads in my brother's car – strange but also lovely. The adult world seemed to be slumbering. Trees twinkled behind net curtains and chimneys belched smoke, but outside it was a child's world made sparkly by the frost. We passed children on bikes and scooters, red-nosed and laughing. We passed others on foot, kicking balls and walking dogs. I felt a rush of emotion on seeing a small boy with black hair and realising I wouldn't see my own child like this. I would just have to imagine it, I thought bleakly.

But Emmie and John's chatter brought me back to the present; it was a real tonic to see them and to have a chance to spend time with them. I had never felt uncomfortable in their presence and they had never been anything but sympathetic and supportive. It was a chance to catch up properly with what John had been up to before being delivered to the less relaxed setting of my mother's house. He had left the army and, following his national service, had returned to his stockjobber firm in the London Stock Exchange, which he told me he was really enjoying again. And Emmie, always so warm and such a friend to me, was her usual bright and chatty self.

I had been right about the likely atmosphere on arrival. As

soon as we went into the house, I felt anxious and uncomfortable. I had not set foot in the bungalow, even to visit, since the previous summer when I'd left to live at June's. I felt disorientated to be there again now. I couldn't quite believe that this would be where I'd be returning after the adoption, that I'd be living here again, with my mother and Sam, just the three of us. It wasn't simply an emotional response: after the Victorian spaciousness of the convent, the bungalow felt overwhelmingly claustrophobic and confined.

I don't think it was any easier for my mother and stepfather than it was for me, and consequently, though everyone was superficially cheerful and cordial, it seemed almost like an out-of-body experience, particularly in my so recently post-natal state.

Paul was on my mind constantly. Presents were exchanged and opened, of course – I got new clothes from John and Emmie, practical slippers and pyjamas and some money from my mother – and I couldn't help wondering: would there be something for me to take back for him? At the same time I already knew the answer to that question. Of course there wouldn't be any presents for my baby. Under the circumstances, it wouldn't have been the right thing to do. How could you buy a present for a child who couldn't even be acknowledged? Whose very existence was a terrible guilty secret? It felt so strange and so sad to be sitting in my own home, with my own family, and being unable to mention the very thing that mattered most to me in the whole world. No one, at any point – not even fleetingly, as I walked in through the front door – so much as asked me how he was.

Were it not for the presence of the 'elephant in the room', it would have passed as a perfectly normal Boxing Day. As I'd not been there on Christmas Day, much of the time was spent on the normal Christmas rituals, such as having a big lunch, followed by the presents, followed by tea, then several rounds of cards.

I'd been told I must be back in the convent by 9 p.m., so we started to think about setting off around 7.30, as we needed to be away by 8 at the latest. John would take me alone, and return for Emmie on the way home. I was getting anxious to leave, in any case, because the image of Paul had been tugging at me constantly, drawing me home to him as surely as if it were his own tiny hand pulling mine.

How would he be? Would he have missed me? Would he be fretful and distressed? I had found it hard to relax, feeling so much like a visitor in my own home, and I was keen to return to the safe, familiar haven of the convent, with its community of other mothers and reassuring routine, where I realised I felt so much more at home. But most of all, I ached for my little baby.

It had long since grown dark, and we'd closed the curtains. When we opened the door, it was to find the road outside cloaked in an impenetrable fog.

'Oh, my,' exclaimed my mother to John, as she looked out. 'How on earth are you going to be able to drive Angela back in that?'

'Dear me,' agreed Sam, coming up to peer over her shoulder. 'That's not looking too clever, is it?'

'I have to get back,' I responded quickly, panicking that they might suggest I sleep there for the night. 'I have no choice.'

'We'll be fine,' John said then, reassuring us. 'Probably just local. You'll see. Soon as we've set off, it'll clear.'

'Are you sure?' my mother persisted. 'It looks terribly thick to me.'

'Yes, I'm completely sure,' he said firmly, and I was so grateful for his firmness. I don't know if he felt as confident as he sounded, but I could tell he sensed my anxiety about getting back to Paul. 'Come on, Angela,' he said, picking up my bag of presents and clothes, and nudging me out through the door. 'Let's get going. Don't want to be late for Reverend Mother!'

But it very soon transpired that we would be. As we drove north, towards the convent, the fog only increased in opacity, and we were reduced to driving along the road at little better than walking speed. After about an hour even John, who up until then had been so sure all would be well, began to express doubts about whether we'd make it.

'There's just no let up, is there?' he said, peering blindly into the white swirls in front of us. He glanced across at me, conscious of me checking my watch every two minutes. 'I'm sorry, sis, I daren't go any faster, I really don't. If there's a car ahead going slower—'

'No, no, that's fine,' I said. 'Just as long as I get there eventually.' I was terrified he'd decide to turn back.

'Oh, don't you worry, we'll get there,' he said. 'Even if it is in the small hours.'

I was so grateful. But I also felt wretched for making him do this for me. This was all my fault, every single bit of it. If I hadn't made the visit, if I hadn't been in the convent, if I hadn't put myself in this terrible situation in the first place . . . But I had to get back. The thought of leaving Paul overnight was unthinkable. However long it took, I had to get there.

The one thing I couldn't bear to do was to telephone and warn them I'd be late, even had we managed to spot a public phone box by the road. Just the thought of their admonishments – 'You should have planned better! You should have thought about the consequences! You shouldn't have been so cavalier! What about your responsibility to your baby?' – was enough to put the idea of phoning out of my mind. It would be crazy to detour to try to find a phone box, in any case. No, better just to get there and face the music.

It was almost midnight by the time the convent finally came into view, appearing like some sort of ghostly Gothic mansion as it took shape beyond the swirling mist. The fog was almost opaque still, but through it we could see the lamp burning above the front door and the glow from an interior light casting a yellowy haze from beyond a window. Apart from that, the building lay in darkness.

I was deeply distressed by now, not only because I feared how my poor little boy had fared without me, but also because I knew that Sister Teresa and the Reverend Mother would both be furious.

I said tearful goodbyes to John – I simply couldn't thank him enough for getting me back – and wished him the one thing he probably couldn't count on: an uneventful and safe journey home.

'I'll wait in the car, though,' he reassured me, having tried but failed to convince me that he should come to the door with me.

I was insistent. He had done more than enough already, I thought, and didn't need a dressing down for his efforts.

While he waited, engine idling, I turned towards the front step and approached the front door, knocking gently at first, and then with increasing strength, as it occurred to me that they had probably given up on me altogether and gone to bed, assuming I'd decided not to bother coming back at all. In which case, I realised anxiously, I could be here for some time, since I doubted if anyone would hear me.

Even though I was expecting Sister Teresa's wrath, I'd under-estimated it. She was almost beside herself with anger.

'Where on earth have you been, girl!!?' she barked at me, her crêpy, wrinkled face almost as white as the mist and her dark eyes flashing daggers as she dragged me inside.

She didn't seem to want to waste time on explanations or recriminations, and immediately dismissed my attempts to explain what had happened. 'I don't want to hear your excuses,' she hissed at me, obviously mindful that we were now inside and might wake people. 'Just go to the nursery and sort out your baby!' she snapped. 'He's been crying all day. All day long, Angela. And all evening, too, and he's disturbing all the other babies. Causing such trouble to everyone! I really don't know what's the matter with him. Now, hurry!'

Why did she need to tell me that he'd been crying all day? It was so cruel, so needless, so unnecessary. And her tone was so mean. It was as if I'd produced some freak of nature, sent to try them and not, as was probably the case, that my baby was just miserable without me and had no other means to communicate that fact. No idea why he was crying? How ridiculous!

I needed no further encouragement to get away from her, and hurried off, as instructed, to take care of Paul. He had indeed been crying. I could see that straight away. His eyes were puffy and his face scarlet. As I picked him up and held him to me, I could feel his little heartbeat, banging furiously against my chest.

I quickly changed him, which helped to settle him, conscious of Sister Teresa's silhouetted presence in the doorway like some grim reaper. I could hardly see, because she'd only allowed me to turn on one tiny lamp, so I settled him with nervous fingers, groping around in the dark. I so wanted to hold him to me, stay with him, tell him I was sorry for having left him and promise I'd never leave him alone like that again.

Once I was done, under the glowering scrutiny of Sister Teresa, I tiptoed quietly up the stairs to the attic dormitory, where I lay down on my bed, still in my coat and clothes, and wept my heart out. I felt exhausted, but my mind was full of guilt. How would I be able to cope with letting another man and woman have my baby? How could anyone look after him as well as I could? My unexpectedly long absence had made the answer painfully clear: no one could.

Chapter Nine

Just as Christmas had, the New Year passed very quietly. It was a day that was spent in much the same way as any other. Though it heralded the start of a new year, all I could think of, as we sat in the common room on New Year's Eve, was how very different it felt from the previous one.

The London I'd known at the end of 1962 wasn't swinging quite yet. It was an innocent time – more like an extension of the 1950s. The clothes were getting more colourful, the pleasures were simple, and the music was upbeat and optimistic. My principal pleasures had been similarly chaste: going to coffee bars, listening to pop music and dancing.

Guthrie and Co.'s offices were on Gracechurch Street, in the City, just a short walk from the River Thames and the Monument. The previous New Year's Eve I'd taken my going-out clothes into work with me that morning; once I'd finished work, Tricia, my closest friend at the time, and I got changed in the office. We often went out straight from work, rather than going home first. Because London is such a big city and many people commuted long distances, it made no sense to travel all the way out and return again.

We rarely ate in the evenings and existed mostly on cake. With luncheon vouchers being one of the perks of our jobs, we'd usually have a proper meal and a pudding at lunchtime. This left us free to spend the evening dancing and having fun. On New Year's Eve, we headed to Trafalgar Square, so we could join the growing throng assembling around the giant tree between the fountains, then as now a gift to London from Norway.

That night I mostly recall laughing as people jumped in the fountain (back in those days it was de rigueur to climb in and splash around) and then losing a shoe when the crowd surged forwards as Big Ben struck twelve. I had a big job on trying to retrieve my shoe before the Tube ride back to Tricia's, in Dagenham, where I often stayed the night.

What a different New Year's Day I'd woken up to the following morning to the one that lay ahead of me now.

Now I was concerned about the immediate future, and how I would get through the next days and weeks. During the first week in January, Pauline, the girl from Cromer, left with her baby Alexander – the son she'd named after Alessandro, the Italian student who had abandoned her to her fate all those months ago. It was a horrible day, and one that would stay with me forever, mostly because of the sound of Pauline sobbing.

I recall sitting in the nursery, doing our morning feed that day, and all we could hear was the anguished sound of her uncontrollable sobbing as she gave him the last bottle of milk she'd ever feed him. I recall the silence, the atmosphere of bleak desperation, and how no one felt able to do or say anything to comfort her – we all knew that no words of comfort were adequate, so it was better to say nothing. And we didn't need to say anything, not really, because we understood how she felt. Our love and empathy didn't need to be made vocal.

But I couldn't bear it. As she was about to leave the nursery, I hastily put Paul down and followed her out. I wasn't sure I'd have another chance to see her before she and Alexander left.

'Oh, Angela,' she cried, turning as I called her name. I spread my arms and she half fell into them, sobbing against my chest.

'Shh,' I said, stroking her hair.

'I can't bear it,' she wept. 'I just want to run away with him. I just want to pick him up and run and run and run. I can't *bear* it!'

I wanted to comfort her, to say something that would make things better, but there *was* nothing. Instead, try as I might to stop it happening, my own eyes filled with tears. 'I'll write to you' was all I could promise her. 'We can be there for each other and meet up when we leave here.' This just produced a fresh wave of sobs.

Sister Teresa appeared then, from the Reverend Mother's office. She didn't speak; she just glared at the two of us, clinging to each other. And her expression was clear: we had brought this on ourselves. If we wanted sympathy, we had better look elsewhere.

Mary was next to leave, only a couple of days later. She had cried so much in the days preceding her departure that she was hollow-eyed and exhausted, and my heart ached for her. And then, all too quickly, it was my turn.

The business of having my baby adopted had been settled a full six months earlier. It had been settled at the time of my relocation to June's house, when I'd signed on with the local GP's practice. It was the GP who had put me in touch with the Social Welfare Department. As a Catholic, my details were then transferred to the Chelmsford Diocesan Moral Welfare Association, a part of the Church that – as was obvious from their title – dealt with such morally sensitive matters. It was through this organisation that I was informed that while, yes, I could go to the convent to have my baby away from the world's disapproving gaze, it was on the understanding that the baby must be adopted.

I had also been given a long list of things to bring to the convent when my place there was confirmed. It was a list that included all the personal items I would need for myself and my soon-to-be-born baby, together with the stipulation that every item be clearly and indelibly marked with the owner's initials – in my case, AMB for Angela Margaret Brown.

The admission letter said nothing about what would happen on adoption day. I knew nothing, therefore, about the logistics of the adoption. I didn't know when and where it would take place, let alone whether I'd meet the adoptive parents. I didn't give the details much thought; like almost all the girls once they'd given birth to their babies, the day of the adoption was something I actively tried not to think about. I would find out soon enough, after all.

It was 11 January when I was called into the offices of the Reverend Mother. I had been in them only once since I'd arrived at the convent, to sign papers confirming that now Paul had been born, I was still going to go ahead with the adoption. At that time it had felt a bit of a blur, but today it couldn't have felt more real or more imminent. As the date of my leaving loomed, I had a knot in my stomach that wouldn't go away, and the sensation of a clock ticking furiously in my head. I seemed to spend half my time praying and the rest dreaming for a miracle, which would mean I wouldn't have to take that fateful journey.

'You're booked in for the sixteenth of January,' the Reverend Mother told me crisply, her voice echoing in the high-ceilinged room. 'We'll be arranging for a car to pick you up around two o'clock.'

I listened silently as she consulted some papers in front of her. 'The car will take you to the Crusade of Rescue in London,' she continued, 'where your baby will meet his new adoptive parents. And you'll be leaving us, too, of course.' She looked up from her paperwork and glanced at me at this point. 'So you'll need to pack your things the night before. Is that understood?'

I nodded, unable to think of anything to say to her. It felt like I was standing before a gallows.

'Oh, and take this,' she said, handing me an envelope, in which I presumed would be the letter that had sealed my fate. 'Hand it in to the Adoption Officer when you arrive.'

I felt numb as I crossed the echoing space back to the door. But at least I remembered to thank her as I left.

*

My bag wasn't too heavy in the end, as I'd given away a lot of what I'd brought with me. I left my maternity clothes – I knew a few of the pregnant girls could do with them – as well as my bed sheets, and quite a few of Paul's baby clothes. After being washed at high temperature in the convent laundry, many of his things were rough and in poor condition. But the nappies and nighties, and the nicer items – the clothes and shawl Emmie had made, certainly – I had put to one side to go with him to his new home. I didn't know whether they would use them – perhaps not – but it was important to me that they should know that the baby they were adopting had been loved and much cherished. If only in a small way, these things were evidence of that love.

I had already given my duster coat to John and Emmie when they'd come to visit, swapping it for something heavier and more suited to the winter, so I left the convent that morning looking ostensibly like my old self, stylish in a black and white check coat with a fur-trimmed collar. Inside, however, I was a shell of my former self.

Every second of that day, till the allotted hour, had been a form of torture, a series of unbearable trials that caused waves of panic to wash over me. I had risen at 5.30, on 16 January, as I normally did, for the first of the day's feeds, my breath clouding in front of me as I left the icy dormitory and gusting in waves over little Paul as I struggled to change his nappy with numb fingers, trying hard not to let my cold hands touch the warm skin of his pink tummy.

I fed him, almost on autopilot, then stumbled back up to bed, where I slept heavily after an understandably turbulent and wakeful night. I had been awake for most of it, praying relentlessly. My prayers had become more desperate as all I could think to pray for was that somehow the adoption wouldn't happen. I kept thinking that now I'd atoned for my sins surely God must have felt I'd been punished enough, surely He didn't mean for me to give up my baby? Surely something was going to happen between now and the appointed hour that would change the course of events so I could keep Paul. It didn't matter how irrational this was. I didn't care. I kept praying over and over and over: please don't take him from me ... please let me keep him ... I'll be a good mother ... he needs me, he needs me ... Over and over and over until I slept. And then I'd wake once more, and repeat it all again.

I woke up groggy and thick-headed for my first stint in the milk kitchen – which today, of course, would also be my second to last. Those tasks performed, it was time for me to give Paul another feed, and to bathe him for the very last time. It would be the last chance for me to feel his tiny naked body against my skin, to clean him, to talc him, to gently rub zinc and castor oil cream into his bottom. I lingered over every aspect of this familiar ritual, fighting back the tears that were blurring my vision, conscious of the other mothers' silent understanding and support.

I tried to commit every detail of him to my memory, knowing that by the time the images began to blur, he would have grown and changed almost beyond recognition. I soothed the redness of his bottom that was the result of having to lie too long in rough towelling, urine-soaked nappies, and fretted anxiously about his unique little foibles and ways. How could anyone but me properly care for him and love him? How could anyone else know him like I did?

With Paul now heavy-lidded and clearly ready for another sleep, I had to put him back in his cot and return to the milk kitchen, going through that other ritual – washing bottles, sterilising them, changing the solution, cleaning the steriliser, wiping down the surfaces, washing the floor – in the same foggy daze as I had prepared the bottles earlier, till the gong for lunch sounded, out in the hallway, at 1 p.m.

'You should eat something,' advised Carol, the sweet girl who'd looked after Paul on Boxing Day, gently placing a hand on my forearm as I joined the short lunch queue. 'You don't know when you'll get another chance to eat, after all.'

'I know. And I will,' I remember answering to reassure her, placing a selection of items on my tray. To this day I have no memory of what they were or what I ate of them, though I do remember pouring myself water from the big Duralit jug, glancing up at the dining-room clock, which read 1.45, and realising I had mere minutes left.

Because the car was due at 2, I had to leave the dining room early, so I made the journey back to the nursery alone. I dressed Paul in the clothes I had brought specially for the purpose, all of them marked, as was everything else, with that carefully inked AMB. I allowed myself to fantasise about the adoptive parents finding out my identity through them, and getting in touch with me to tell me how my son was getting on. It was a faint hope to cling to. How could anything like that possibly happen? It would be the last thing they'd want, surely? But I clung to the idea anyway, because it helped.

Paul was almost fully dressed when Linda joined me in the

nursery. As she'd promised, she was clutching her black and white Polaroid camera. The Polaroid, back then, was a very new-fangled thing, which actually took photos *and* developed them all at once. She had kindly offered to take his picture for me, as she had for Mary. While I untied the blue weight chart from the bars of his cot and slipped it into my bag, she took the photograph and pulled it out of the front of the camera.

We huddled close as the image started to develop out of the blackness. 'Take good care of it, mind,' she said as she handed it to me. 'Or it'll scratch. And don't put it in your bag until it's completely dry, or it might stick itself to something and be ruined. Here,' she said, tears welling in her eyes, 'let me take it. You've little Paul to hold, haven't you?'

She carried my bag too, and together we made our way out into the hallway. I could see from a small window that the car had already arrived. At almost that exact moment, Sister Teresa appeared from the dining room and called to me to hurry up.

Linda helped me, carrying my holdall out to the car, with me following behind, Paul in my arms. Our goodbye was tearful but hurried; even as we embraced, I could hear Sister Teresa telling her to go back inside.

I got in the car then, still carefully clutching my baby and my damp photo. My last view of Loreto Convent was a glimpse of Sister Teresa's swishing habit as the heavy wooden door closed behind her. I hugged Paul tight to my chest as the car crunched over the gravel and away. The time for prayers was finally over.

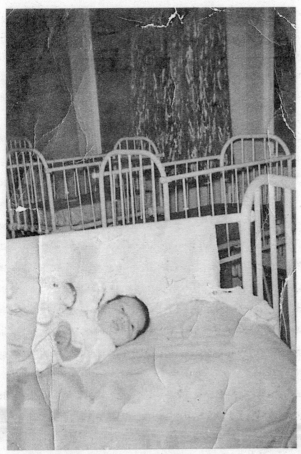

My precious photo of Paul as a baby.

Chapter Ten

The offices of the Crusade of Rescue, the charity that had organised Paul's adoption and were today going to carry it out, were based at 73 St Charles Square, in Ladbroke Grove, West London, and the journey, the driver told me, would take around an hour and a half. The full name of the organisation was even more emotive: written properly, as it had been on the papers I'd signed for the Reverend Mother, it read 'The Crusade of Rescue and Homes for Destitute Catholic Children' – which said it all, really. I had needed rescuing from mortal sin, and they were now about to do that, and my baby, nestled in my arms and sleeping peacefully, would surely have been destined to become destitute were it not for their kind and timely intervention.

They meant well, I was sure, and had only the best of intentions. They were, after all, operating in a very different world to the one in which we live now: a world in which the contraceptive pill wasn't yet generally available and countless women risked their lives – and sometimes lost them – having crude backstreet abortions; anything was preferable to being pregnant and unmarried, or married but pregnant by another man. For those girls for whom illegal abortion was not an option – girls like me, practising Catholics – the only alternative was to give the baby up. And if that *was* your only option, which it mostly was, then it was important to be sure that the new parents would be people you could trust to do right by your child and bring up him or her according to your faith.

Perhaps, my addled brain kept suggesting, they wouldn't like him. Perhaps they would take against him, for some reason or other, and what was surely going to happen wouldn't happen after all.

But still we journeyed on, getting closer to our destination. I had no idea where in London we were going, what route we were taking, or what was going to happen when we got there. I felt as I had during the latter stages of my pregnancy: unable to focus on the reality of what was happening, and drifting off and creating ridiculous scenarios in which my fate would be different.

I had prayed so hard, as I had never prayed before, to God and the Virgin Mary, to Jesus, St Anthony and St Teresa, pleading with all of them to show me some mercy and find another way for me to pay for what I'd done. I didn't care what. Nothing could hurt me more than separation from my son. Any fate, any punishment would have been preferable to this one. To have this baby, *my* baby, taken away from me would be an enduring punishment. I couldn't see a future in which I would be healed of the pain. But my prayers had not been answered, so today I had to give him up, and all I could do was try to bear it.

As we made our way from the wintry rural solitude of Theydon Bois towards the teeming and brightly lit bulk of my beloved city, I tried to think about what the parents chosen for Paul might be like. Though it was almost impossible to think of another woman holding him, mothering him, taking ownership of him, there was a part of me desperate to be reassured about her, too. What would she look like? Would she be gentle? Would she be warm and responsive? I didn't even know if I would get to see her, let alone speak to her. But if I did, what would she think of *me*?

We arrived at around 3.30 in the afternoon and I finally put away the Polaroid picture, slipping it into the envelope in which I'd put the cot card. I'd had almost no conversation with the driver, a taciturn middle-aged man from the local taxi firm, who had probably made this journey many times before and from whom I'd sensed a kind of grim-faced but unspoken acceptance that this wasn't the time or place for chatty small talk. I wondered what he thought of all the girls and babies he ferried here. Did he judge us as harshly as we judged ourselves?

He let me out onto the wide residential road, came round to open the rear door of the car and nodded silently. The buildings opposite were imposing four-storey Victorian terraces, their frontages almost all identical. Each had steps, whitewashed walls, big bay windows and an air of opulence; they seemed to look down on me, in every sense. In front of me huddled a group of low-level, modern buildings, which looked incongruous in this elegant place, and were mainly hidden behind a high brick wall. The street was tree-lined on both sides, and the bare winter branches formed a spindly canopy above us.

Clutching Paul in the crook of my right arm and my big holdall with my left hand, I followed the driver through the gateway to the buildings, where he pushed open a door to let us through. He seemed to know exactly where he was going, confirming my thought that he had done this many times before.

'Good afternoon,' said a lady, who was standing behind a big reception desk. 'You have a letter?' She looked at me enquiringly.

I put down my holdall – the driver had disappeared back through the door – and pulled the letter from where I'd stowed it in my coat pocket. Paul stirred very slightly but didn't fully wake as I did this. The woman at the desk barely gave him a glance. I wondered what it must be like to *be* her. To spend much of your working day dealing with ashen-faced young women, like me, clutching babies, and then watching them leave empty-handed. To spend the rest of the day in the company of new adoptive parents, taking those same babies off to new lives. Had she become immune to the extremes of emotion she must encounter? Did she feel anything?

She took the letter and read it, and I decided from her expression that what she probably felt most was that she was doing the right thing. She then turned back to me. There was no hostility in her features, but there was no smile of sympathy either. 'Come with me,' she said. 'I'll show you up.' I picked up my bag and followed her.

The room she showed me into was high-ceilinged and bare of adornments. It was clearly a waiting room, as it contained a low table on which an array of dog-eared magazines was scattered, and a number of assorted wooden chairs. 'Just wait there,' she said, closing the door behind her.

It was opened again, only a few moments later, by another woman, this time younger – perhaps only in her twenties – and much more welcoming. 'Hello. I'm Miss Whiteley, the Adoption

Officer. And you're Miss Brown, yes?' She approached now, looking smart and businesslike. 'And this will be Paul?'

I nodded. I was beginning to feel numb. 'Yes, it is.'

'And how was your journey here?' she asked, as she peered at Paul. 'Did he sleep all the way?'

I nodded again, touched at her interest. 'Yes. Yes, he did.'

'Right,' she said, waving an arm towards the chairs along the wall. 'Sit down. Make yourself comfortable. I'll be back with you in a few minutes.'

I put my bag down beside one of the chairs, and settled Paul and myself on it. He was still fast asleep and I was torn between my natural desire to leave him settled and peaceful and my need to spend some last precious time gazing into his eyes. His lashes, so dark, brushed his cheeks as he slept, and I contented myself with gently smoothing his velvet-soft skin with the side of my little finger, feeling his warmth and drinking in the smell of him.

I had been sitting there for about fifteen minutes before Miss Whiteley returned. It felt like longer, which for some reason made me feel anxious – what was happening? At the same time, it meant cherished extra moments together. She entered the room again, leaving the door open this time, her mouth forming a smile as she approached. 'I'm just going to take him to show him to the couple,' she said, proffering her arms to take Paul from mine.

The couple. It made my heart thump. 'Okay,' I said, rising and handing him to her trustingly. His eyes flicked open at the movement and looked straight into mine, but soon closed again, as he sank almost immediately back into sleep, as young babies do.

Miss Whiteley smiled again. 'I'll be back in just a minute,' she said.

More time passed, only this time I imagined it would be shorter. Remembering the little bag of baby clothes I'd brought with me, I bent down and opened my holdall to retrieve it, ready to hand it over on their return. It was then that I made the decision to keep Paul's rosary for myself, so I removed it from the package and slipped it into a side pocket in my handbag.

I was curious to know what the couple's reaction would be on seeing my beautiful baby. Then I heard an exclamation – clearly one of delight – in a female voice, so I assumed it was the adoptive mother's. Good, I remember thinking proudly, despite the lump that had lodged in my throat. They must have really liked him. I sat back down on the chair and continued to wait.

But then the door, which had been ajar, opened again fully to reveal Miss Whiteley, now empty-handed. 'They think he's lovely,' she told me, once again approaching my chair. I stood up then, as if to attention. Where was Paul? 'And he's got *such* a lot of hair, hasn't he!' she said. 'Are these his things?' She gestured towards the bag of clothes beside my holdall.

I had no words. I couldn't answer. I had completely lost the power of speech. Was that *it*? Wasn't she bringing him back to me to say goodbye first? 'Thank you. I'll pass these on,' she said, answering my unspoken question. So it was true. They had taken him. She *wasn't* bringing him back. I felt tears flood my eyes. Why hadn't I realised she would do that? Why hadn't someone *told* me this was how it would happen? She'd said she'd be back in a minute, hadn't she? She'd said, 'I'll *show* him to them', not 'I'll *give* him to them', hadn't she?

I felt all hope drain from me. Was that *really* it? My stomach turned into a cold, cavernous pit in that instant, and it felt as if my heart had dropped into it. That *was* it. I'd been denied saying goodbye to my baby, denied that last chance to stroke his cheek and feel his fingers grip mine, to kiss his tiny mouth in loving farewell. Why hadn't she *told* me I was never going to see him again? Why hadn't she told me it was time to say goodbye to him? I'd thought she was just going to *show* them, not let them *take* him. Why hadn't she said? Oh, why hadn't she *said*?

Miss Whiteley smiled at me again, but it was a much smaller smile this time, one that seemed to say that this was how it worked, this was what was best for me. 'Thank you,' she said again, coldly, as she bent to pick up the carrier bag. 'I'll make sure they get these right away. And, well, please do sit for a moment if you need to. You can go when you're ready.'

Ready? I thought. *Ready?* How could a person *ever* be ready to do something like this? How could you ever be *ready* to give up your baby?

Miss Whiteley left the room then, and returned to the adoptive parents. I knew because I could hear them talking together, only now in low voices, tempering their obvious delight as if being mindful of the occasion, almost as if they were peripheral guests at a funeral who must take care to show respect to the bereaved.

As I stood there my body became animate again, twitching back to life, and with the life came the pain building and building, like a great rush of pressure, till I became racked with unstoppable, shuddering sobs. My baby was no longer mine. He was theirs. It was over. And I knew I'd never feel whole again.

I looked up at the clock on the wall as I left. It was 3.50 on 16 January 1964. It was a date and time I'd never forget.

THE CRUSADE OF RESCUE
and Homes for Destitute Catholic Children

I Angela Margaret Brown of Loreto Convent

hereby request that my child Paul Brown be admitted into the care of The Crusade of Rescue to be brought up in the Roman Catholic Religion. I furthermore give my full consent and agree that the Administrator for the time being of the Crusade of Rescue may place the said child at any time he may think fit either in a Children's Home or Boarded Out with a Foster Parent as may be considered desirable. And in consideration of the said child's admittance I hereby agree that the said Administrator shall have the powers of a legally appointed guardian of the said child and I undertake not to interfere in any way with the said child Paul Brown while under the care of the said Administrator and will not remove or attempt to remove the said child from his custody without his permission.

(Signature of Parent) A M Brown.

Date 17th December, 1963.

(Signature of Witness) M. Sylvester M.S.C

Date 27.12.63

I also agree and consent to the child being under the general care of the Society's Medical and Dental Officers and receiving from time to time such medical and dental and other treatment, and, in particular to receive :—

1. The administration of gas for dentistry.
2. Preventive inoculation where necessary in an emergency.
3. The administration of any anaesthetic.
4. Such operation, surgical or otherwise as is considered necessary or desirable by a Medical Officer.

it being understood that the Administrator will make reasonable efforts to notify me of any intended treatment and provided, however, that no major surgical operation shall be performed and no general anaesthetic shall be administered without my prior consent to the particular operation or administration of a general anaesthetic unless the case is one of such urgency that the delay in obtaining such consent might endanger the life or health of my child.

(Signature of Parent) A M Brown

(Signature of Witness) M. Sylvester M.S.C

THE CRUSADE OF RESCUE

Telephone:
LADBROKE 2803, 6, 7, 8 & 9

and
Home for Destitute Catholic Children

REGISTERED ADOPTION SOCIETY   INCORPORATED 1945

Administrator: Very Rev. Canon CHARLES S. FLOOD
Assistant Administrator: Rev. PHILIP HARVEY

Registered Office:
73, ST. CHARLES SQUARE,
LADBROKE GROVE, W.10

Your Ref.   Our Ref.

ADOPTION ACT 1958

Particulars relating to Infant
(to be completed by the mother of the child)

Name   PAUL BROWN

Date and place of baptism   30-11-63 — LORETO CONVENT, EPPING.

Religious persuasion of the infant's father and mother   ROMAN CATHOLIC

Name, address and age of the infant's father and mother

MOTHER ANGELA MARGARET BROWN   FATHER ▓▓▓▓▓▓▓▓▓▓
42 DANBURY ROAD
RAYLEIGH, ESSEX — 20 YEARS.   LONDON ▓▓▓ — 21 YEARS

If either is dead, date of death _____

The age and sex of any other children _____

I hereby declare that

There is no history of tuberculosis, epilepsy, mental illness or
other disease in my family   NO

As far as I know there is no history of tuberculosis, epilepsy,
mental illness or other disease in the family of the father of
the child.

I am offering my child for adoption because   I am unable to provide a
comfortable   and   suitable home.

I have not/offered my child for adoption anywhere else   No

I was/was not married to the father of my child.

The father of my child does **not** object to adoption.

My child has no guardians other than myself and only I have any right and
powers as parent.

My child does not own or have interest or right to property and I have/not
taken any insurance policies on the child's life for any purpose whatsoever.

Signature... A.M.Brown ....   Witness... M. Sylvester, M.R. ....

Date...17th December 1965.   Rank... Rev. Mullin ....

I left the offices of the Crusade of Rescue in the same sort of
daze I'd been in on the long journey there. The day was clear,
growing dark now, but I was only dimly aware of it, because I
seemed to have lost my mind. For some time I just wandered

from street to street blindly. I didn't know where I was, much less where the nearest Tube station was. I kept ploughing on, though, under tree after tree, crossing roads randomly, not even looking. All I knew for certain was that I had lost my beloved child and I was never going to see him again.

Eventually, after something like an hour or so had passed – I recall seeing a clock – I recognised the lights of an Underground station, and wandered in, my holdall now a dead weight on the end of my arm. I then got on a Tube train, though I didn't know where it was going and I didn't care. The train was really crowded, with everyone strap-hanging and jostling. As I looked at the mostly expressionless faces, I thought, '*You have absolutely no idea what I have just had to do.*' Eventually, the train reached some stations I recognised, and I stayed on it till it pulled into Liverpool Street, my connection to the mainline and home.

Home, I thought, as I now shrank into a seat on the packed commuter train, hoping desperately that I wouldn't chance upon any previous work colleagues and holding my holdall tight against my chest. Home. The concept of 'home' felt very alien. Apart from the visit on Boxing Day, I hadn't returned 'home' since June of the previous year, and it didn't feel like home any more. So much had happened to me. I'd had to cope with so many monumental, life-changing events all alone that I felt detached and disconnected from my mother and stepfather.

It was dark by the time the train reached Rayleigh, the sky inky and star-spattered and the temperature bitingly cold. I walked for five minutes along the familiar route to the bungalow, and was soon staring, sightless, into the curtained front rooms that sat beyond the empty flowerbeds. I stood and stared for some minutes, unable to find the strength to go in. How could I come back here? How had my legs brought me here? It felt as if everything that had happened had been leading to this moment, this moment when I must mentally let go of my baby and slip quietly back into my old life. Except how *could* I? I wanted to scream. I was in agony.

I opened the gate, walked up the path and pressed my finger against the doorbell, my breath making loose skeins of mist in the night air. My thoughts centred on the sickening apprehension I felt about what kind of reception I might get after all these months away. But even in my traumatised, distressed state, I could not have anticipated the response I *did* get.

'Oh,' said my mother, opening the door to greet me. 'You're here. Would you like some dinner?'

I lay on my bed for an hour. Having told my mother 'no', I went straight to my room and lay down on the bed, exhausted, fully clothed and prostrate with grief. But the oblivion I so badly craved eluded me. It felt so strange to be lying here alone, with nowhere else to go and nothing to distract me. There were no bottles to sterilise, no jugs to be collected, no interminable wait on a musty thin mattress for the next time I'd be allowed to go down to the nursery and drink in the scent of my crying infant – nothing. I badly missed the comfort and solace of the other girls. How would I get used to this? How would I bear it? Compared to the pain of childbirth, which had been intense and considerable, the pain of my heart shattering was as physical an agony as I'd ever felt before, and I didn't have a clue how to ease it.

I knew then that I would never find peace. I would never find a way to be reconciled to my loss. The pain would never diminish. It would be there for all time, like a stain I would have to live with – one that never washes away and colours every-thing.

My mother, perhaps wisely, stayed away from me. I could hear the normal house sounds but felt removed from them, sep-arated by an invisible barrier. I wasn't sure I would ever feel 'at home' here again – not without my little boy. I was no longer the same person who had left all those months ago. I was a mother now. But unlike my own mother, who had known the joy of rais-ing her children, I was a mother without a baby.

After a while, I realised that there was an answer. If I could die, then I wouldn't be in pain any more. I got up and quietly crept into the bathroom. I had hoped for a bottle of pills of some sort, but all I could find were half a dozen paracetamol. I took four of them anyway, but then hesitated. What on earth was I thinking? I mustn't die. To die would only make certain what was at present only probable. If I died, I would *definitely* never see Paul again; if I lived, there was a chance, albeit infinitesimal, that I might. That thought allowed a seed of hope to grow. There might be a very small chance of somehow seeing my son again; although it was improbable, the possibil-ity was there. And that possibility wasn't important just for me: if I died, he would never be able to see *me* again, either. I was his mother. If he ever needed me, then it was my *job* to be there.

I slept then, still in the clothes I had dressed in back at the convent, and I didn't stir until the next morning. When I did, one thing was clear: I wasn't ready to face the day, much less the rest of my life, but equally I couldn't stay in that bungalow.

Chapter Eleven

My mother was finding it as difficult to cope with things as I was. I didn't blame her. It didn't matter how much hurt I had inside me or how much I wished she had felt better able to support me: the 'sin' was mine, so the consequences were mine to bear also. But I felt so alienated from her. I knew she wouldn't understand the pain I was in – how could she? – but she seemed not to be making any effort to, either. I had to pretend nothing had happened; I wasn't able to acknowledge it, talk about it or explain quite how much I was hurting and missing Paul. My head was teeming with a cacophony of thoughts and feelings, none of which I was able to share with her. I couldn't bear the atmosphere this created between us, and I craved the supportive company of the girls in the convent, who had been through the same experience and understood.

I was also awkward around my stepfather, and he around me. We'd never been close, Sam and I, initially because he hadn't understood teenagers; now he didn't have a clue what to say to me.

It was John and Emmie who came to my rescue. Just a week before I'd left the convent they'd moved house. Since John had finished his national service, they'd been living with Emmie's widowed mother in Dagenham, but now they'd bought their own place in Eastwood, just outside Southend-on-Sea.

'Okay if I come in?' Emmie asked, a few days after my return. She and John had popped over for a while, and she'd come to my bedroom, where I was now spending most of my time. I was feeling paralysed by grief and increasingly disinclined to leave the room, even though I knew the isolation was probably the last thing I needed. Tormented by my loss, my room was the only place where I felt I could just be me, and I would spend hour after hour staring sightlessly at the posters on my wall. They were prints of modern art mostly – stylish, quite sophisticated, but now they seemed to belong to another life.

I tried to read: *The Best of Everything* by Rona Jaffe. But even though I felt a kinship for Jaffe's heroine, Caroline Bender (her mother's sage advice was similar to that of my own – 'don't let boys touch you'), her life and world now felt very distant from mine. The outside world, generally, felt hostile and alien. No one knew what I'd been through and, even if they had, they wouldn't have cared.

I nodded. If there was one person I could talk to, it was Emmie. She gestured to the bed, where I was lying, listlessly trying to read my book, and sat down beside me.

'Your mum's worried about you,' she said. 'I know it might not seem that way, but she is.'

My expression must have suggested that I wasn't convinced, but she wasn't having that. 'She doesn't really know what to say to you,' she continued. 'That's the problem. And how can she, after everything you've been through?' She lowered her voice. 'And let's face it, she has no *idea* what you've been through. None of us do, do we? But, well, you know your mum. It's especially hard for her, because she feels . . . well, it's difficult for her to talk about, isn't it? Sooo,' she said, her tone changing now, 'we've hatched a plan between the two of us. How about you come to me and John for a bit?'

'What, now? You've come for supper, haven't you?'

Emmie shook her head. 'No, we're off soon, I think,' she said. 'But I didn't mean for supper; I meant to *stay* with us.'

I pulled myself up onto my elbows. 'To stay?'

'Yes, to stay.' She smiled. 'Don't look so surprised. It's not going to be the Ritz, I know, and, no, it doesn't have a sea view. But we're still close enough to smell the ozone.'

'Oh, Emmie, I'd *love* to. Thank you *so* much.'

'Okay, steady on. Don't get carried away. You've not seen the "to do" list I've drawn up for you yet. You'll have to earn your keep, you know. I've got a lot of boxes that still need unpacking. So there'll be no time for lying around feeling sorry for yourself.'

I couldn't have been more grateful. I could sense the cloud lifting already: I could get away to somewhere entirely new, where I'd able to talk to someone who was happy to *let* me talk. 'Leave them *all* for me,' I said, sitting up and putting my arms around her neck. 'Anything you need doing, *really*, I'm happy to do it. Oh, this is so kind of you, Emmie, I can't tell you.'

'Don't be daft,' she said. 'It's all a ruse to get some work done around the house. I just booked two weeks off work, and want some company that's a little more entertaining than an emulsion brush.' She stood up. 'Plus the sea air will do you a world of good. You're so pale, you look like you've been living in a cave with a load of trolls.'

I swung my legs around and stood up too. 'So when can I come?'

'How soon can you get packed?' she replied.

I was never party to their conversation, but I found out later that my mother had been very worried about me, traumatised and depressed as I so clearly was. So she had confided in Emmie, and they had indeed hatched a plan. So for all my upset at her inability to give me the emotional support I needed, at least I knew my mother cared.

It was such a comfort to get right away from home and spend time with Emmie. She was so kind, and having taken two weeks off work just to be with me – something I only found out later – she looked after me in every way possible. Though the January winds bit and the sky remained as dark and gloomy as I felt, we spent many, many hours sitting on the promenade at Southend and walking along the local seafront, stopping for endless lunches and cups of tea and coffee.

'So tell me more about that dreadful convent,' she'd demand. 'Such a grim and gloomy place! I nearly died at the thought of you locked up in there with all those ghastly nuns!'

And off I'd go, telling her about the milk kitchen and Sister Teresa, and how we'd shiver in our dormitory and swap our tragic tales. It was so therapeutic to *tell* someone. I showed her my little Polaroid of Paul – up till then not a single soul besides Linda and I had seen it. I described every detail of his foibles and little ways: how he'd been, the things he did, the way he'd looked so lovely in all her outfits. And I recounted every detail of the day I'd travelled into London and handed him over to Frances Whiteley, which was still so raw and painfully clear in my mind.

Sometimes we didn't talk much at all. We'd just walk along the prom, arm in arm, saying nothing, because sometimes it was too difficult for me to speak. Other times we talked about my elder brother, Ray, wondering about the changes in his life since he'd returned from South Africa, and about his and Jean's children, Sean and Lynne, now both gorgeous toddlers. He had a business set up here now, which was already doing well, and we agreed how nice it was to have the family together again.

It was good to be able to talk about the future, because I needed to accept and embrace that there was one, for Paul with his new family and for me. I couldn't hide away and nurse my broken heart forever.

I left Emmie and John's feeling so much stronger, and determined to get back to work. I needed occupation for both my mind and my body. I knew it was important that I try not to dwell endlessly on my loss. So I called Bunty, my former boss, and to my great relief she urged me to return right away.

But it wasn't simply a case of returning and slipping quietly into my old life. I'd been gone for eight months and it felt like a lifetime. And, more importantly, in terms of the welcome I received, they were eight months during which I'd ostensibly been having the time of my life.

'Ah, the wanderer returns!' was the first greeting I was met with when I entered the office. 'So,' everyone seemed to want to know, 'was it fun?'

Though Bunty knew the truth, as did my friends Doreen and June, no one else at the company knew what had happened to me. As far as everyone else knew, I had just returned from my extended spell in Italy, where it was assumed I'd had lots of exciting adventures.

This left me on tenterhooks for weeks. 'You must bring in some photos,' demanded Barbara Walton, as soon as she saw me. She was the MD's secretary, and was always very chatty. I often bumped into her because we both worked on the same floor. It was obvious she wanted to know all about my trip. 'I've been thinking of going to Italy this summer,' she said, catching me in the corridor. 'Where did you stay? Can you recommend it? It would be brilliant to see your snaps.'

'Er, Laigueglia, it was. And I'll bring them in,' I told her. 'Tomorrow, I promise.'

And I kept promising to bring them in, over and over, in what seemed like a constant round of interrogations about why I'd forgotten them yet again. I became expert in the art of bluffing, fielding difficult questions with off-the-cuff fabrications, and ducking out of conversations that threatened to get tricky by suddenly needing to be somewhere else.

It was so hard trying to keep up the pretence and appear jolly, but not as hard as it was to cope with the weight of my loss. Despite my determination to try to get back to normal, I still felt depressed and empty – hollowed out inside – and thoughts of

Paul and how he was faring were constantly at the forefront of my mind, but I had no release for them. Apart from Emmie, there was no one I could talk to about him. Though my friends at work were sympathetic, I knew I couldn't burden them with it. They didn't want to hear my woes all the time, did they? And, besides, as soon as anyone *did* talk to me about it, I seemed incapable of preventing the tears from coming.

I was on the verge of crying every time I so much as *thought* about Paul, so I constantly had to try to shut out those thoughts and keep my head firmly fixed on my work. For that reason, and also because I felt so at odds with the world now that I carried such a big and dreadful secret, I clung to the friendship I'd made with Pauline at the convent. With Pauline, at least, I could talk about Paul without worrying she'd get distressed if I cried. So we'd talk on the phone and we'd sob to each other. The pain was no less, but when I talked to her I felt a little less alone.

But I *was* alone, in the sense that mattered most to me. I had had a child and that child was elsewhere, with a different family, being loved and cherished by people other than me. But how *was* he? Was he coping okay without me? One thought that kept surfacing and wouldn't go away was how bewildered he must be about where I'd gone. Did he cry for me a lot? Did he miss my smell and touch? All those days and weeks of his new life when it had been just me and him – surely he must be feeling my absence?

I also ached – physically ached – to touch and hold him again, and felt so wretched to think he would forget me. I prayed he wouldn't, but I knew that *of course* he'd forget me. He was so tiny. I wouldn't even be a memory for him. Just one more time, I kept praying. Let me see him one more time. Just give me one chance to hold him and tell him that I love him.

I had at least been able to give him one lasting thing: he still had the name I'd chosen for him. I became fixated on knowing his adoptive parents hadn't changed it, hadn't taken away that one thing he had from me. And, luckily, I had a chance to find out.

One evening in late February I was visited at home by a Mr Hasler from Middlesex Probation Service. It was Mr Hasler's job to help me fill in and sign all the legal papers, ready for the adoption to take place formally in the courts at the end of March. He was a nice man, quite formal, but approachable and kind. I didn't know if it was allowed, but I had nothing to lose, so I asked if he'd be in touch with the adoptive couple himself. He told me that, yes, he certainly could be.

'So, do you think,' I asked him, 'that you could perhaps ask them a favour? Could they perhaps send me a photo, so I can see how he's getting on?'

'I don't see why not,' he said, noting it down on his pad.

'And could you maybe also ask them about his name?'

'His name?'

'Whether they kept it as Paul? That was what I asked for, before they took him: that they didn't change his name. Could you check that too, do you think?'

'Of course,' he said, smiling sympathetically, as he made another note. I wondered if he had children of his own.

And less than a week later, true to his word, he had done it.

I now had another photo of my precious baby. It was only a head and shoulders shot, but I could see he was already much fuller in the face. I was grateful to see evidence that he was being fed properly and no longer had to survive on the convent's meagre rations. It was also such a comfort to know that my wishes had been heeded and he still had the name I'd given him.

After that, I could only wait for the formal adoption to take place, and while I did so I tried hard to move on. I could remain trapped in misery or I could try to move forwards. I resolved to try to halt the tide of despair that kept threatening to drown me. No longer was I going to lay bare my emotions about Paul. Instead I would consign him to a safe private place in an innermost sanctum of my mind.

PART TWO

Chapter Twelve

'You know what I think we should do?' said Pauline. 'I think we should go to Blackpool for a holiday.'

It was the beginning of May 1964, a Saturday, and she'd travelled up to London so we could spend the day shopping and doing a bit of sightseeing. We'd been spending a lot of time together lately, and had a really close friendship. We both found comfort in the fact that, for the two of us, Paul and Alexander were able to exist. And though we consciously tried not to dwell on our losses, it was such a relief to be able to talk about our babies instead of pretending they'd never been born. We were in Regent's Park today, wandering among the throng of weekend crowds, many of whom flocked here to meet Guy the gorilla, one of London Zoo's most popular attractions.

'Blackpool?' I said. 'Really?' The thought of going somewhere like Blackpool would never have entered my head. I'd spent most of my childhood going on caravanning trips to the quiet spots my parents preferred, such as St Osyth and Clacton and Jaywick Sands, but after my father had died, there'd been no further family holidays. Bar the trip to Italy, in recent years the only place I'd been was Ireland, to stay with my mother's relatives. And right now the thought of going away *anywhere* hadn't occurred to me. I was just living day to day, getting through.

'Yes, Blackpool,' Pauline said, grinning at me. 'And don't look so shocked. It's brilliant there, such fun. And it would be such a tonic for us both. I can probably find a good place we could stay, as well – nothing too expensive, obviously. My parents will know somewhere, I'm sure.'

Pauline's parents ran a bed and breakfast in Cromer, and apparently knew lots of other people in the trade. 'Wakes Week, I was thinking,' Pauline went on. 'Because it will be really lively then, won't it? What d'you say? Do you think you could get the time off from work?'

Wakes weeks were still quite common in the 1960s. They were designated weeks during which all the mills and factories in an area would close so the workers could go on holiday. The late May one was common in the north-west of England, particularly Lancashire, and crowds would flood to the coast, mostly to Blackpool, because of the beach and the famous funfair.

I thought for a moment. Why *not* go to Blackpool? No, it had never occurred to me before, but at the same time I couldn't think of a reason to say no.

'I could try,' I said. 'As long as I'm quick, I expect I can. It's not a particularly busy time at work, I think.'

'That's settled then.' She squeezed my forearm. 'Oooh, how exciting! Trust me,' she added, 'you will *love* it.'

*

I don't know what I expected to find in Blackpool. I had only the usual stereotypical ideas about what it might be like: fish and chips, stripey rock, donkey rides, 'Kiss me quick' hats and so on. As soon as we arrived, almost all the stereotypes were confirmed. I didn't actually see a 'Kiss me quick' hat that first day, but I certainly saw donkeys, fish and chip bars and sticks of Blackpool rock aplenty. There were also typical British holidaymakers in droves: men with trousers turned up so they could paddle in the sea, and elderly ladies, their stockings rolled down, huddled in deckchairs, hunched low to avoid the fresh wind that blew in off the North Sea.

It was everything I had anticipated, but also something more: it felt happy and alive and inclusive and full of warmth. As we made our way from the North Station to the bed and breakfast Pauline had found for us, I knew it had been the right decision to get away somewhere like this. It felt so good to be away from everyone and everything familiar, and had done the minute our train had rolled out of King's Cross.

Pauline's parents had put us in touch with a couple who ran a small place a short walk from the seafront, where they'd stayed, years back, when they'd first gone into the business themselves. It was one of a row of almost identical Edwardian terraced houses, with a neat front garden, enclosed by a low, whitewashed wall. There were heavy net curtains at the double-fronted bay windows, in one of which hung a plastic 'No Vacancies' sign. The whole house, you could see, had been recently painted sunshine yellow – perhaps an optimistic nod to the coming season.

'Welcome!' said the proprietress, opening the front door

wide to usher us both in with our cases and giving us a warm, ruddy-cheeked smile. 'I can see you two girls have brought the weather with you, too. Come on in. That's the way. Let me show you upstairs.'

Having booked so late, all that had been left was a cramped bedroom at the back of the house, but it would do us fine; we didn't plan on spending much time there, after all. And it was a lovely afternoon, so we didn't linger, just staying long enough to change out of our travelling clothes of capri pants and sleeveless blouses and into light cotton summer dresses. We then headed straight for the pleasure beach and pier, drinking in the sweet scent of candyfloss.

The place was packed, as Pauline had predicted, the promenade crowded with smiling holidaymakers. In the throng it almost felt as if we were exactly what we looked like: two carefree single girls out to have a good time, which – for small pockets of time anyway – we were.

And we didn't go unnoticed. By lunchtime on the fourth day, after a leisurely morning sunbathing, we'd decided to go bowling on the pier. We'd already sampled some of Blackpool's more famous attractions: we'd been to the funfair, climbed the tower, ridden donkeys on the sand. We'd also made a special point of visiting the vast Tower Ballroom, not to dance but to take in the awe-inspiring enormity of it; up till now we'd only glimpsed it on *Come Dancing* on television. But we particularly enjoyed the bowling alley when the sun got too hot, and we were both getting quite good at it.

We'd only just taken possession of our lane and got settled when Pauline nudged me hard in the ribs. 'Angela,' she hissed, putting her face close to my ear. 'Look who's over there! See? To your right!' She jabbed a discreet finger towards a nearby lane, where two young men had just arrived. 'Isn't that Jimmy Tarbuck over there?'

I turned and looked. It *was* Jimmy Tarbuck. Or at least it certainly *looked* like Jimmy Tarbuck. I recognised the trademark gap in his front teeth. But like anyone seeing a famous person in the flesh, especially somewhere you didn't expect to, I wasn't sure I could believe my eyes. And he *was* famous – unquestionably. He was one of the new rising stars of variety at that time, and seemed to be everywhere you looked. Plus (and here I realised that, of course, it was Jimmy Tarbuck) I remembered he was appearing in Blackpool that week. We'd both seen the posters – even commented on them. And here he was, going bowling, it seemed. I didn't recognise the other guy he was with, but just then he looked across the lanes and caught me staring.

I quickly went to pick up my first bowling ball. 'Yes, it is,' I told Pauline, feeling my cheeks begin to redden. I took a run up and launched it down the alley.

'Ladies!' called a male voice from over to our right, as I watched it roll. 'Hello!'

Pauline and I turned around simultaneously to see Jimmy Tarbuck now gesticulating at us. I was conscious that in the lanes between us – there were three of them – all activity had stopped. At the same time a rumble of whispered conversation had begun.

'I'm Jimmy,' he called obligingly, ignoring it. 'And this is my friend Roger,' he added, gesturing to the other guy. 'We were wondering – would you two like to make a foursome?'

Pauline and I glanced at each other.

'How about it?' he continued. 'We thought it might be fun – what do you think?'

'Hi there,' called Pauline, always slightly bolder than me. They were making their way around the back of the lanes to where we were. 'I'm Pauline,' she said. 'And this is Angela. Pleased to meet you. And, well, yeah, why not? What d'you think, Angela? Shall we?'

Roger, Jimmy told us, was the stage manager at the theatre where Jimmy was performing that evening – one of several along the pier – and they were whiling away a few hours before getting ready to do that night's show. Needing no further encouragement, they joined us in our lane. After losing graciously to us, the two of them suggested we take a stroll back to the theatre with them.

'You can meet Mike and Bernie,' Jimmy added gaily. It wasn't necessary to add 'Winters' when he said this: at the time, the brothers, who performed as a comedy double act, were almost as well known as he was.

We set off in pairs, though it soon became obvious that being famous was something of a full-time job for Jimmy. He walked slightly ahead of us, smiling and waving, acknowledging each ripple of recognition and adulation not with any arrogance – he didn't seem like that at all – but certainly with a great deal of pleasure.

That we *had* paired up was clear, and flattering, though the concept of pairing up with anyone didn't come naturally to me any more. I hadn't 'paired up' with anyone for over a year. The last boyfriend I'd had was Peter, Paul's father, and the whole business was one I wished only to forget. Though I felt a little nervous and apprehensive about being flirted with so energetically, not to mention slightly awed by it being by someone so famous, I found myself quite enjoying the sensation.

Equally enjoyable was walking along the pier that afternoon and getting something of a taste for what fame might be like; warmth and affection seemed to accompany Jimmy everywhere. Not that, up close, it seemed in the least surprising; he came across as a friendly and approachable star. And perhaps now, I mused, I'd have some real anecdotes to tell everyone at work. It wasn't every day you got chatted up by a television personality, after all.

And there was little doubt that I was being chatted up, as was Pauline, because once we'd said hello to Mike and Bernie Winters in their dressing room (where Mike Winters was strolling around, rather disconcertingly, in a pair of arrestingly tight Y-fronts) Jimmy suggested I go back to his dressing room with him for a while. 'I want to be out of the way before Norman bloody Vaughan turns up,' he whispered, as he steered me by the elbow down the long corridor. 'Can't stand the man.' By this time Roger had already disappeared with Pauline to take her on a 'short tour of the theatre', or so he'd said. It was therefore either that or, well . . . that. And I was having fun, so why not?

Jimmy's dressing room was fairly spartan, and not at all starry. There were none of the embellishments I would have expected: no light-bulb-rimmed mirror, no chaise longue, no cards and flowers. Not that I would have noticed much – I was too overawed and preoccupied. 'Tell you what,' he said, after I'd deflected several enthusiastic attempts to kiss me. 'How about you girls come back after the show? There's a cabaret starting at 11.30, straight after. We could go together. The Bachelors are playing. I could get you and your friend put on the guest list, if you fancy coming along. What do you think?'

He grinned his gappy grin and attempted another kiss. I didn't doubt he could have any girl he set his sights on. But I didn't mind. He was entertaining company.

'I think that sounds great,' I told him, deflecting the kiss. But I did really mean what I said – he was nice, and I liked him, and I was enjoying the attention. It meant nothing, I knew, but it seemed like such a long time since I'd felt anything remotely like the young, unattached girl I was, such an age since I'd last felt pretty. I was carrying around so much heartache, it weighed me down.

'Brilliant,' he said, angling in for another kiss and smiling broadly. This time I decided I would let him.

'So what do you think?' Pauline asked, once we'd said goodbye to the guys and were ambling back along the pier after our unexpectedly interesting afternoon. She'd had the same invitation from Roger, she told me, and we both wondered, giggling, if they had been in cahoots.

But back out in the sunshine I was beginning to have reservations about the wisdom of meeting up with them again later. It was one thing to be kissed, quite another to get involved in late-night trysts.

'I'm not sure,' I said, tentatively, trying to assess Pauline's feelings. 'I mean, in some ways, I'd like to, wouldn't you? You know, go and hobnob with the stars . . .'

We both laughed. 'I can't believe I've seen Mike Winters in his pants!' Pauline said, grimacing. 'Not a sight I shall easily forget. And it'll certainly be one to tell them back in college!'

'And I can't believe I've been kissed by Jimmy Tarbuck!' I agreed. 'Who'd have thought it?'

'But it'll be pretty late . . .' Pauline said. 'And it's not like they've invited us to the show even, is it?'

'I was thinking that, too,' I agreed. 'Though it's probably already sold out. So we'd just be hanging around all evening, wouldn't we? And then . . .'

'And we know what they'll be after, let's face it,' she said. 'God, more wandering hands than an octopus, that one!' Pauline pulled a face again, and I didn't blame her. I hadn't much liked the look of Roger myself. He was a bit older, and a bit too forward as well.

'I did wonder,' I said. 'Plus it occurred to me that just by *going* there to meet them, it would be giving them the impression—'

'*Exactly*,' she agreed, finishing the thought for me. 'Giving them the impression that we're up for something more than we really are.'

We'd reached the end of the pier now, and the beach was beginning to empty. Ahead of us, the lights along the prom were coming on, punctuating the backdrop with arcs of white join-the-dots. I tried to imagine myself at the stage door of the theatre at 11.30, waiting to be taken to a cabaret by one of the stars of the moment. Pauline was right. That would definitely be one to tell my friends back in the office. But it didn't feel right.

I stopped and turned to Pauline. 'I think we'd be out of our depth a bit, don't you? And once we're there . . .'

'I was thinking the same thing,' she said.

We didn't really need to discuss it any more. We both knew exactly what 'out of our depth' meant and what it could lead to. We'd been there and well knew the consequences.

We went out for fish and chips instead.

Chapter Thirteen

With the exception of Pauline, I rarely mixed socially with girls of my own age. I was still just twenty, yet I felt older and, as a consequence, disconnected from my peers. I had become someone different; someone who carried a dark secret. It seemed better to strike out and find new friends than to keep up the pretence with the group of people who'd known me and my baby's father.

Not a day passed in the aftermath following Paul's adoption when I didn't think of him, but as the weeks turned into months, and the pain began to quieten a little, I grew less introspective and once again interested in rejoining the world.

And the world seemed quite happy to accept me. Though I still had the jitters when going out, always dreading the thought of being exposed, there was clearly something about me that boys now found attractive. I had no idea what it was – a sense of vulnerability? A mystique? I couldn't understand why, and I wasn't about to analyse it, but for a while I was constantly turning down offers; offers, moreover, from really nice boys. Boys who I was sure wouldn't look at me twice if they knew the truth about what had happened to me.

There was one in particular, a good-looking boy called Andy, whom I'd been interested in for months before the night I'd met Peter, and with whom I'd had no success at all. But that had changed. I would often see him at the Meads Ballroom once I started going there again, and soon became aware that, for reasons I couldn't begin to fathom, it was he who'd become interested in me now. Being asked out by Andy should have been a thrilling moment – eighteen months ago, it would have been – but it wasn't. Somehow he'd lost his appeal. Either that, or I'd changed more than I realised.

I'd made another good friend now, a girl called Janice. A couple of years older than me, she was the daughter of my friend Doreen's neighbour. Our paths had never crossed before, but I think Doreen sensed we'd be kindred spirits – she'd recently parted from her fiancé after things had gone wrong between them, so, though for different reasons, she too was 'recovering'. She knew nothing of what had happened to me – as far as she knew, I'd been out of the country – but that aside, we grew close very quickly. She was tall and very pretty, but she lacked confidence in herself. She was shy and always easily embarrassed. I suppose, looking back, we supported each other through a time when we were both finding it hard to socialise again.

But, little by little, we did socialise more. Buoyed up by one another, we started going out regularly to the popular clubs of the day. There were exciting new ones opening all the time. As well as the Meads Ballroom, we started going to the Rhinegold and the Marquee in London. We weren't exactly living a hedonistic high life, because that was the last thing I wanted, but I did have the sense that I was, albeit tentatively, resuming a version of my former life.

We continued to meet boys, and I still loved to dance with them. In some ways life felt as if it was slowly reconfiguring itself. I was finding my feet again, regaining some much needed confidence. But I turned down all dates – it was almost an automatic reflex – and, like Janice, I invariably went home alone. I still felt I couldn't get close to anyone of the opposite sex, because becoming intimate with a boy would mean telling him the truth. To be close to another human being you had to open up, to give your *whole* self – otherwise what was the point? I couldn't bear to do that. Not yet, at any rate. My secret felt much too shameful to share.

But, by increments, the world was changing too – for the better. Out of necessity, I'd spent much of the previous year looking inward, but now I could see evidence of the dawn of a different era, of a society that was perhaps becoming a little less judgemental. If the period that preceded it had seen the world shocked by John Profumo, 1964 marked something of a turning point, to my mind.

It was the year the *Sun* newspaper was launched and the death penalty was abolished, and there was a constant sense that the old order was being challenged and swept away. Attitudes to sex outside marriage had slowly begun to change and, at least for those not hidebound by the rules of the Catholic faith, use of the pill was becoming widespread, as women took control of their contraceptive needs. It would take many years yet, but it felt like a sea change was occurring all around – confirmed that autumn when thirteen years of continuous Conservative government ended and Harold Wilson's Labour party took power. And the soundtrack to *everything*, both here and in America, was provided by that new band we'd been so excited by in the convent – Liverpool's greatest export, The Beatles.

It was also the year in which I turned twenty-one, and my mother was determined that we should celebrate. 'We want to organise a party for you,' she told me, unexpectedly, when I returned from work one evening in the September.

I was shocked. My mother wasn't the party-giving type, and neither was Sam. The last party they'd had anything to do with, as far as I could remember, was when they'd celebrated their own wedding. But Sam was kind, and I knew he'd do anything for my mother – he adored her – so if she'd decided upon a party, I knew he'd support her. Even so, it was unexpected. 'A party?' I parroted. 'What, *here*?'

'No, not here,' my mother said, shocking me even further. 'Sam and I have discussed it, and we thought perhaps the best thing would be to see if we could hire the Oakwood Rooms in Eastwood. What do you think?'

This, too, may have seemed unprecedented, but, looking back, it might not have been such an out-of-the-blue suggestion as it appeared. I knew my mother was anxious to make things right between us. There was also the small matter of me having a boyfriend at last, my first since Peter, who seemed so very long ago. And he wasn't just any boy, he was – to use my mother's parlance – a very *nice* boy.

He was called Dave, and I'd met him at the Meads Ballroom; he'd made a beeline for me as soon as he'd seen me. This time I'd said yes, because he'd ticked all my personal boxes. He was tall – very important – and a very smart dresser; as with Peter, my late father would have approved. He also wore his hair, which was dark and wavy, in the way that I liked it – slightly long and with a quiff at the front. He was a draughtsman, and I'd been seeing him for something like six weeks. My mother and Sam definitely approved of him. She would comment often, and with increasing regularity, I'd begun to realise, on what a wonderful husband he would make.

I could understand her enthusiasm. Not only was Dave a 'catch' in every sense you could think of, but he also represented the potential closing of a very harrowing chapter in my life. I could see what she was thinking: once I was safely married, she would no longer have to worry about me, which was something, since 'getting into trouble', that weighed heavily and constantly on her mind.

I didn't mind. Dave was nice, and I enjoyed his company. It was also a pleasant sensation to feel wanted by someone. That he was keen on me wasn't in any doubt. In our short relationship we'd even got a song to call our own: 'I'm Into Something Good' by Herman's Hermits, which had come on the radio when he was dropping me home one evening, and which he declared to be exactly how he felt about me.

'Really?' I said to my mother now, genuinely excited. 'I would love a birthday party, I really would!'

She smiled indulgently, and I wondered how hard she'd had

to work to persuade Sam that this was something they should do for me. 'Good,' she said. 'Then you shall have one!'

The Oakwood was a lovely venue close to where John and Emmie lived, and everyone chipped in with the preparations. They did wonderful food there, and I have lots of happy memories of that time, as we gathered as a family to work out all the details: what the buffet menu would be, what music we'd like the DJ to play and exactly which family and friends to invite. We even had the invitations specially printed, which made me feel very much the belle of the ball, in stark contrast to my twentieth birthday.

I would look the part too, hopefully, after my mother agreed to put money towards having an outfit specially made for the occasion. It was a deep pink dress, made of the fabric of the moment – Moygashel, a type of heavy Irish linen. It had a fashionably high neck and cut-away shoulders, a keyhole back and a stylish A-line skirt. It was short, so I could make the most of my best asset, my long legs, and was finished off with a neat boxy jacket. I felt a million dollars in it. When the night of the party came around, it was clear Dave thought I looked a picture too.

'You look amazing,' he told me, as we jigged around the dance floor together. I had by now, as ever, taken my shoes off. 'And you know who you remind me of?' he said. 'Sandie Shaw.'

I smiled at this, even though it was a bittersweet moment, as I remembered a similar conversation a long time back. But Dave, unlike Peter, *did* have a point. Sandie Shaw was the latest 'big thing' girl singer, and her recently released single, 'Always Something There to Remind Me', was currently storming up the charts. Like me, she had long dark brown hair and a fringe, and was generally seen barefoot.

But it wasn't really Sandie Shaw who was on Dave's mind that evening. 'I've got a surprise for you,' he said, as the song we'd been dancing to ended. He gestured to the DJ, who gave him a nod, and then Herman's Hermits came on. I could see my mother sitting at a table at the edge of the dance floor, and her expression as she watched us spoke volumes. She was sitting with Sam, of course, as well as John and Emmie, and my auntie, and I could tell they had been commenting on the two of us dancing – conspiratorily, as they were all beaming. And as Peter Noone began warbling, I had a moment of real panic. Oh, no, I thought. He's not going to propose, is he?

Dave didn't propose; he was just pleased that he'd arranged for the DJ to play 'our' song for us. But it was at that moment that I think it really hit me: as much as I liked him – and I did because he was so nice – we were probably going nowhere as a couple. Dave was lovely, and I knew my mother had plans for him, but in that moment of panic at the thought of a declaration, I also knew the spark wasn't there. However suitable, however much *he* thought he was into something good, Dave wasn't going to be the man for me.

I knew it was going to take a very special kind of person before I would even *think* about sharing my dreadful secret, before I would contemplate allowing someone else to know my pain at losing Paul. Dave wasn't that person. That person might not even exist. The truth was that I might *never* find him, and if I didn't so be it. It had to be the right man or no one. Dave and I finished seeing each other not long after.

Chapter Fourteen

B ut potential happiness lay just around the corner.

My brother John often went to Catford Cricket Club at the weekends. A friend of his from the Stock Exchange, called Terry, lived in South London and was a member there. John and Emmie would often go with him to the social evenings they put on, and they would talk about them often – how much fun they were, and how much I'd enjoy them. Eventually I was persuaded to join them, along with Janice, on one of their Saturday night outings. More often than not they were themed in some way: Caribbean, perhaps, or French, with similarly themed food and entertainment, and people would be encouraged to dress up for them. On this occasion, however, there was no theme and, as it turned out, no occasion either.

It was 6 February 1965, a bitter night. And suddenly we were all dressed up with nowhere to go. 'Cancelled?' said John, when we arrived at the club to find the car park almost empty, no sign of Terry and the door to the function room shut.

'Yes, sorry about that,' said the man manning the reception. 'All a bit short notice, I'm afraid; one of those things. Though there's a band playing in the pavilion a bit later.' He spread his hands in apology. 'If you've nothing better on, that is.'

Not too enticed by this lukewarm endorsement, John turned to us and spread his own hands. Terry, it seemed, had been off work sick on the Friday, and the news about the cancellation, as a consequence, hadn't filtered through. But we didn't have anything better on, and we were now in Catford, a long way from our usual haunts. 'Great,' he said. 'What shall we do instead, then?'

Emmie, always the optimist, headed for the door to the pavilion. 'Well, we might as well at least go in for a drink, mightn't we? Who knows? The band might be brilliant.'

We followed her and poked our heads through the open door. It was the standard issue cricket pavilion of its day: a long bar, wooden floor, some chairs and tables. The four members of the promised band, who looked as if they were probably drawing pensions, were setting up their equipment in the corner. 'Hmm,' said John, voicing all our thoughts about the evening's prospects. 'Okay, then. One drink and we'll make a new plan.'

For me, it was the best decision ever.

Well, the second drink was, at any rate. We had decided upon having another once a few more people had arrived in the pavilion. It had livened up a bit as a consequence, and now we were settled no one had much enthusiasm for moving on, particularly as it was such a cold night.

'Ah, there's Michael,' John announced, seeing an obviously familiar face at the other end of the bar.

'Michael?' Emmie asked. 'I don't recognise him. Should I know him?'

John shook his head. 'No, you wouldn't. He's a friend of Terry's,' he explained. 'Works for another firm of stockbrokers. I see him on the floor sometimes.' He turned towards me and Janice with a twinkle in his eye. Like me, Janice was still single, and my brother wasn't averse to a spot of matchmaking. 'Shall I ask him and his friend if they'd like to join us?' he asked. 'Since we're staying now, we could get ourselves a table, couldn't we?' He pointed. 'You want to grab that one over there?' He winked at me as we crossed the noisy floorboards in our heels. 'Who knows,' he said. 'They might take a fancy to you two!'

Emmie rolled her eyes at me. 'Men!' she observed. Yet, my brother, for all his indiscreet attempts at getting me hitched, served me well. The two men came and joined us, and introductions were made. Dave, an old school friend of Michael's, made a beeline for Janice, while Michael, it seemed, was immediately drawn to me. And the feeling was mutual. He was instantly engaging, with sandy hair, a touch ginger (though I soon learned he hated it if you called it that), and good-looking, too, with arresting blue eyes. These he trained on me now, most disconcertingly.

He was dressed smartly, in a navy mohair suit that fitted beautifully, over a button-down shirt and slim knitted tie. The whole look gave the impression that, just like us, he'd originally had more exciting plans than standing in an almost empty cricket pavilion awaiting the opening number by a quartet of septuagenarian musicians. And it seemed he had; he hadn't known about the cancellation either, so, like us, he'd planned to move on.

Though now, he said, it looked as if he might be staying. He had spotted me, apparently, as soon as he'd walked in, and he wasn't slow in letting me know it. His chat-up line was to take a measured look at me – we were around the same height – and make me an offer. 'If you promise to take those off,' he said, nodding towards my black patent shoes, 'I'll have a dance with you later.'

'Is that right?' I said, coolly. Privately I was impressed by his acuity. Were we to stay the whole evening, I would be doing that, for sure. But I would enjoy teasing him a bit first. 'Well, we'll see, shall we?' I finished.

He grinned. 'Will it help if I tell you it's my birthday?'

It wasn't his birthday. When pressed, he admitted that it was still ten days away. But it seemed he wasn't about to let a little detail like that put him off. And soon it became apparent, as the place filled up even more, that everyone was quite happy staying for the evening, me very much included. The band started, I duly slipped off my shoes and we danced.

It felt nice. We made a date for the following weekend. He asked if I'd like to go and stay with him for the weekend, in fact, which rang sufficient alarm bells that it almost scuppered our fledgling romance before it started. What did he take me for?

'Angela, he's *fine*,' John was quick to reassure me on the journey home.

'If a bit cheeky,' I said.

'Yes, but it's not like he was suggesting a dirty weekend, or anything. He lives with his parents, doesn't he?'

'Yes, I think so. But even so . . .'

'Honestly, sis,' John said. 'He's a decent guy, trust me. Straight as they come, promise.'

And he was right.

But Michael wasn't interested in waiting till the weekend to see me again. He called me on the Monday evening, very keen to meet up, and we went for a drink after work at a pub near Liverpool Street station on the Wednesday. When the weekend did come around, he suggested he could drive me down to meet his parents. The family had recently moved from South London to a new home in Crayford, in Kent, and they would, he said, really love to meet me.

This is too soon, I remember thinking on the way down to see them. This was all happening a bit quickly. Much as I liked him, I was in no rush to get serious with anyone till I was sure, and meeting his parents felt like a giant step. Meeting a man, and going out with him, was scary enough in itself.

I was a naturally honest person and it was bad enough dealing with the amount of subterfuge in my life already; the thought of having to tell my secret to someone important to me still hung heavy. He doesn't know me, I kept thinking. He doesn't know who I really am, or what has happened to me. And he would need to. Yet the thought of that happening was stupefying.

In hindsight, my anxiety about having to open up to Michael was probably an indication that my feelings for him were already much stronger than they'd been for Dave. And there was no doubt that Michael was serious about me – he made that very clear from the off. He wore his heart on his sleeve. He'd told me he loved me and intended to marry me on our second date, and though we both laughed (in my case, in a somewhat shocked fashion) I got a strong sense that he absolutely meant it. I didn't know how he could be so sure how he felt about someone he'd only just met, but it was one of the most attractive things about him. I loved his impulsiveness, his confidence, his happiness in his own skin, his lack of guile. But it was also terrifying to know just how strong his feelings were, because if there was one thing I didn't want to do it was to play with or be cavalier with his emotions.

Only a couple of weeks later, it hit me. I had to end things. I couldn't bear the weight of my secret, and it was beginning to make me panic. I really liked him, and that was why I needed to finish it. I had to protect myself – and him – and walk away. It never occurred to me that there was an alternative. Once he knew the truth about me, he would obviously want to end it. Better to do it now myself than make things worse.

We'd just left the pub when I decided I had to do it. It was a place called the Square Rigger, on London Bridge, where we'd met up after work for a midweek drink. It was a chilly night, and I had my coat wrapped tightly around me, my hands clasped together at the neck, keeping the cold out. Michael's arm was linked through mine, making its presence felt, even though neither of us had spoken for some minutes. I felt determined in that instant. I couldn't keep this going. I felt too much for him already. And he clearly felt the same about me. Why prolong the agony? I needed to do it now.

We were heading for Monument Station, and I could see it

fast approaching, so I stopped in the middle of the pavement. There were still lots of people around, hurrying to wherever they were going, but the bridge itself was as good a place as any to face the music. I couldn't look at him. If I did, I knew I wouldn't be able to say it.

'I think I need to end this,' I blurted out, before I could change my mind.

Having delivered the words, I wanted nothing more badly than to run away, but I couldn't. He stopped too, pulling up sharply beside me. His arm slipped from mine. He looked stunned.

'What?' he said. '*Why?*' His expression was understandably horrified. I'd given him no clue this was coming. But how could I? I'd known myself only moments ago.

I couldn't seem to order the next words I needed to say to him.

'*Why*, Angela?' he said again. 'Don't you like me any more?' His expression was still one of incomprehension. I had done nothing, said nothing, to prepare him for this.

'It's nothing like that,' I said, anxious to reassure him. He looked so crestfallen. 'It's me,' I explained. 'It's all about me.'

'What about you?'

'Something in my past.'

'What something?' he began.

'Something I should have told you from the outset,' I said, 'but didn't. I'm so sorry, Michael. Something I've done. Something bad.'

'Bad?' he looked confused now. 'What can you possibly have

done that's bad?' His expression shifted then. 'Is it someone else?'

'No! Not at all!' I said. '*Nothing* like that!'

He looked relieved now. 'Fine, then. So I don't need to know, do I? As far as I'm concerned, what's past is past, okay? It's not going to make any difference to me, trust me.'

I shook my head. 'No, Michael. You're wrong. It *will*. It's too big. A really big thing—'

He grabbed my hand. 'I don't *care*, Angela,' he said. 'I really don't. Everyone has things in their past. *Everyone*.'

He has no idea what's coming, I thought. Not a clue; not an inkling.

'Not like this,' I said quietly, blinking away the tears that had now come. 'Michael, I've had a baby,' I said, enunciating the words slowly and carefully. 'I've had a baby and he's called Paul and I had to give him up for adoption. Last year. Last January.'

I explained what had happened through a mist of hot tears. Michael took my other hand and hung on tightly to it as I told him. His eyes never left my face as he listened. His expression never wavered. 'I *told* you,' he said finally, once I'd finished. 'It makes no difference to me. It doesn't matter. It wouldn't *ever* make any difference to me. You must know that. *Surely*?'

'But it *must* do,' I persisted. 'Michael, *listen* to me. I've had a *baby*. You can't possibly want to be with me now you know that—'

'Angela, you're not hearing me. *Nothing* could be further from the truth, okay? Nothing. I love you. You know that. You do know that, don't you?' He looked so upset himself now, as if I'd

offended and hurt him by even suggesting he'd want to finish
with me. Seeing that made me cry more. He's not taking this in,
I thought. The problem is that it hasn't hit home yet – the enormity of it, the implications – but it will. Once he's had a chance
to sleep on it, of course it will.

'But what about your parents?' I said. 'What are they both
going to *think* of me?'

I had met his parents twice by now, and I liked them so much,
particularly his mum, who was so different from mine. She'd
seemed so bubbly, so welcoming and so much fun to be with. It
wasn't that my own mother was cold or unwelcoming, it was just
that Michael's mother, so much younger and so much less con-
strained by religion, seemed as if she came from a different, more
accepting generation. But then she didn't know the truth about
me yet, did she? It hurt so much to think she must have thought
I was one thing and now she'd have cause to look at me in a completely different, damning light.

Michael shook his head. 'This is nothing to do with anyone
but you and me,' he answered. 'This is about *us*. Not my parents.
Why do they even need to know?'

'But—'

'Angela,' he said, pulling me close. 'We don't need to *tell*
them. Not if you don't want to.'

'But they have to *know*.'

'No they *don't*. Nobody *has* to know anything. They really
don't. And shall I tell you something else? If you did tell them,
it wouldn't matter to them either. I know it wouldn't. I know
there are people in the world that like to stand in judgement over

others, but my parents aren't like that. And neither am I. There but for the grace of God, frankly ...' He looked exasperated. 'Please don't tell me we're finished, okay?'

'But—'

'Just don't tell me we're finished. I love you. I don't care about any of what you've told me. It makes no difference to me, okay? None at all.'

This was such a shock to me. How could that be? I had spent so long hanging my head in shame, so long carting my status as a fallen woman around with me like a ball and chain. And I'd seen so much evidence of society's disapproval. I'd had to scuttle away from work, lied and been shunned by so many people. I'd had it drilled into me, again and again and again, that I had sinned, I was a sinner, I'd got myself into trouble, and the world had every right to disown and look down on me.

How could he stand there and say what he was saying? He couldn't mean it. He just couldn't. He wasn't thinking straight.

'But how can it *not* make a difference?' I said.

He grabbed my other hand then, and kissed me. 'It makes *no difference*,' he said again. 'And I'm not letting you go into that station till you promise you believe me.'

'Okay, I believe you. But—'

'No buts. Just promise.'

'I promise.'

'Okay,' he said. 'In that case you can go and get your train. And I'll call you tomorrow, and I'll tell you again. Just don't end this, okay, Angela. Please.'

So I promised that, too, and he let me go and I got the train and travelled home, my mind a blur of anxious thoughts. Perhaps he *was* telling the truth. Perhaps right now it *didn't* matter. But then, realistically, he probably hadn't taken it in yet. All I could do now was wait and see.

Michael called me when I got home from work the next evening, just as he'd promised he would. The phone was ringing as I walked through the front door. 'I've been awake half the night,' he said, without preamble. 'I nearly called you at five this morning before I left for work. I've been going mad all day, Angela. *Mad.*'

'I'm so sorry,' I said. My stomach lurched, hearing his voice. 'I hardly slept either. I wouldn't have minded if you *had* called.'

'I wish I had! Because I kept going back to the same question,' he went on. 'How could you *think* that? That's what I kept thinking.'

'Think what?'

'Think that about me – that I'd treat you like that. That what you told me would make the slightest difference to how I feel about you? I've been running it round and round my head, and I'm still in shock. How could you *think* of me that way? That I'm someone for whom something like that would *matter*? I feel the opposite, if anything. Just thinking what you've been through. I'm so *angry* for you, Angela. I really am.'

I felt so chastened, hearing that, almost as if I'd compounded my original sin. At the same time, my heavy weight had been spirited away from me. I realised then just how anxious I'd been about hearing from him, despite trying so hard to convince myself that I wouldn't, that he'd be the one walking away.

'I obviously don't know you as well as I thought I did,' I suggested meekly. 'I'm so sorry, Michael. I—'

'Exactly,' he interrupted. '*Exactly* what I thought. So you obviously need to get to know me a lot better, don't you?'

And now I would. I could. I put down the phone that evening feeling different. Feeling that, actually, my life might turn out okay after all. But mostly, as the days passed and turned into weeks, I felt something new and wonderful. I had that bubbly feeling in my tummy every time I thought of him. I would wish away the hours between the times that I'd see him. I was oblivious, suddenly, to the world trundling on around me. And I knew why. I'd found the person I wanted to spend the rest of my life with and it was Michael.

I had fallen in love.

Chapter Fifteen

Michael and I were married on 12 March 1966, in Our Lady of Ransome Catholic Church in Rayleigh. It was a place with connections to both of our families, as the priest who married us had gone to school with my brother Roy, and his sister was one of Michael's work colleagues.

We had nothing when we married and we couldn't have cared less. We had a roof over our heads, albeit a cramped and grotty one. It was the back half of the top floor of a terraced house in Ilford, and we shared a bathroom and toilet with the young couple at the front. The owners, who lived downstairs, weren't old, but they were old-fashioned: bedtime was 11 p.m., and if we made any sort of noise after that, we would invariably get a sharp rap on the door. In fact, we spent most of our time there creeping around very carefully, as the aged floorboards protested at our every step. We had no proper kitchen either, and used to do our washing up in a washing-up bowl, perched awkwardly on the sink in the bathroom.

For all that, it was a time I recall with much joy. I had left home and, in doing so, had separated myself from all the bad things that had gone before. On the surface, life at home had already returned to normal. Indeed, my mother was very happy to see me married to Michael. She genuinely liked him, and I knew she was relieved, because she no longer needed to fear that I might 'get into trouble' again.

I'd also separated myself, if not from the constant yearning for my lost baby, at least from the stigma of the event that had caused me so much unhappiness. I had a future now, so I could look forward without fear.

Our honeymoon, out of financial necessity, was short. But we didn't care about that either. We were just happy to be together. We packed up Michael's Ford Cortina and embarked on a mini road trip, spending our first night in Cambridge, then driving on up to the coast to King's Lynn, before returning to London. Our last treat – and my favourite – was a visit to the Ideal Home Exhibition, where we drooled over all the things we couldn't yet afford. We agreed we'd definitely have some of the teak furniture – it was terrifically fashionable at that time – and, naturally, we'd accessorise in lurid oranges, olive greens and purples, those colours being the height of sophistication. And we did make a start, with what little money we could spare; we bought a teak salad bowl with stylish matching servers, together with a bread knife and bread board that we still use today. But mostly we just looked, and dreamed of our future.

Happily, a matter of months later, we had a stroke of good fortune. My brother Ray, whose business had been growing steadily, opened a new shop in Seven Kings. He already had a shop selling car parts in Chadwell Heath. With the phenomenal popularity of the recently introduced and now ubiquitous Mini, he'd spotted a gap in the market. The new shop would deal exclusively in parts and accessories for Minis; it would go on to do well for many years, expanding into a successful export business.

But it was the spacious flat above the shop that meant so much to Michael and me. Having agreed terms with my brother, we took it on to rent, travelling there every evening after work, over a period of several weeks, to make it liveable. Yes, we were miserable having to go back to our 11 p.m. curfew, but like any young couple we were also thrilled beyond belief at the thought of finally having a proper place to call home, even if, for the moment, we would have to be patient about that teak and make do with a few sticks of hand-me-down furniture.

Hard up as we were, Michael and I were like-minded. One thing we were determined to save up for was a proper foreign holiday, and in August 1967 we headed off for a fortnight in Ibiza, my first time abroad since my teenage trip to Italy.

The Mediterranean back then was just becoming fashionable as a destination for British holidaymakers, and I was really excited at the prospect of flying somewhere so exotic. Michael, being three years older, was more travelled than I was: whereas I could count only Italy and Ireland as my other 'foreign' holidays, he'd already been to several places in Europe, including Luxembourg, Holland and Belgium.

Even so, we were happy to be shepherded by a tour operator — in this case, Clarksons, one of the main companies selling package holidays, at that time an increasingly popular way to travel. We left from Southend Airport, by charter flight, on an overcast

Saturday morning, and though the hotel was a bit grotty and our room was without a view, Figueretas, where we stayed, had everything we wanted: lots of sunshine, a lovely beach and a chance to relax properly.

Not that we wanted to spend the whole time on sunloungers – we were also keen to get out and explore the island. There were apparently empty beaches to be discovered all over, even at the height of the season. Our first plan when we arrived was to go and see if we could hire a scooter to venture a little further afield.

The first night, however, we stayed close to home, sitting outside a bar, chatting to another couple till the early hours – a novelty in itself – before going on to a nightclub, where we danced almost till dawn. We were up late the next day, and it was only then that I realised that I'd forgotten to pack something fairly fundamental.

'Oh, dear,' I said to Michael, after a protracted and fruitless search through the jumble of our belongings. In the rush to go out, we'd unpacked a bit haphazardly the evening before. 'You'll never guess what I've forgotten to bring.'

He groaned theatrically. 'Oh no! Not the toothpaste!'

I couldn't help but smile, for our pre-holiday advice had been clear: toothpaste was one thing we mustn't forget to bring, as for some reason it was difficult to come by. I shook my head. 'No. But actually it's worse: my contraceptive pills.'

'Oh,' said Michael, coming in off the little balcony and adopting a thoughtful expression. 'So what can we do about that, then?'

Michael being a practical sort – and I could see his mind working now – would, I imagined, have some sort of practical solution. Doubtless he'd suggest that we go and find a *farmacia* somewhere and attempt to make our pharmaceutical needs known, though this was Spain, a Catholic country. I didn't fancy our chances, even with the help of the big English/Spanish dictionary that I had obviously been much more conscientious about packing.

'Well . . .' I began, about to suggest, but then dismissing, the most obvious solution: a fortnight of abstinence. I smiled ruefully at him. 'Not a lot, I think,' I finished.

But he surprised me. 'So,' he said, plopping himself down on the bed beside me. 'It'll just have to be a case of *qué será, será*, I suppose, won't it?'

'*Really?*' I must have looked as shocked as I felt, because he put an arm around my shoulder and squeezed it.

'It would hardly be the end of the world, sweetheart, would it?'

I brightened. 'It wouldn't?'

I was surprised, because we'd already talked about this. We knew when we wanted to start a family: when we could afford it; when we'd bought a house; when we were ready, which wasn't quite yet, and we'd both agreed to that. However much my heart craved the joy of holding a child of my own in my arms again, this time I wanted the circumstances to be perfect.

'No. I mean it wouldn't be *ideal*, obviously,' he agreed. 'We don't have our own home yet, for one thing. But we'd manage. I'm sure we would. How hard can it be, after all?'

He had a twinkle in his eye and I loved him for it. John and Emmie had just had their first child, a little girl – she'd been born on the day after our first anniversary, in fact – and it had been both moving and funny to see how Michael was with her. As an only child, he'd had little experience of babies, and just as I'd been when I had Paul, he was very nervous. He'd eyed her warily, then picked her up as if she was a piece of expensive china or an alien – one who might do something terrifying at any moment. I no longer had that beginner's anxiety. And the thought of being related to this perfect tiny human had not only filled me with joy, but also confidence, because holding her and caring for her felt as natural as breathing. Yes, Michael was right: it wouldn't be ideal for us to start our family just yet. Though it would be a struggle financially, as far as 'managing' went, I had no worries whatsoever. We'd be *fine*. I said so.

'And can you imagine how thrilled my parents would be?' He rolled his eyes. We both knew how much it would mean to them. 'To get their hands on their first grandchild?' He smiled broadly at the thought. 'Trust me, you'd be having to beat my mum off with a stick!'

This was to be a thought, and an image, that would stay with me for a long time. What a wonderful notion – to have a baby who'd be so loved by all the family.

'It's all hypothetical anyway,' I said, though I'm not sure whom I was trying to reassure most. 'It's not like it's a given . . .'

'Exactly,' Michael agreed. 'So we'll not worry about it, eh?' I nodded. He stood up. 'That's henceforth the official plan, then,' he said. 'If it happens, it happens. If it doesn't, it doesn't. *Qué será, será.* Lap of the gods. Come on. Let's go hire that scooter and get this holiday properly underway.'

But I didn't return home pregnant, and I wasn't sure what to feel. I stopped worrying about it, certainly, once we'd had this conversation; instead I'd thrown myself into having a lovely time. Though it did cross my mind at odd moments – we were on holiday, so it felt romantic – it would be a lie to say I had started consciously hoping that it would happen. The timing wasn't right, and we both accepted that quite happily.

Even so, when my period came just after we returned, I felt an unexpectedly powerful pang of disappointment. It would have been nice, we both agreed. It wasn't to be, but it would have been *so* nice to start our family. I went back to taking the pill, as per our original plan, and we put all our energies into saving for the house we both so wanted. Once we'd achieved that, we agreed, we'd start trying properly. I'd get pregnant, I remember thinking confidently, soon enough. After all, I thought, look how easily it had happened to me before.

But God, it seemed, wasn't done punishing me.

We'd found our new home the following summer, in the pretty little town of Tenterden in Kent. It was a gorgeous mock Georgian house, detached, with three bedrooms. Once we'd moved in, I stopped taking the pill, just as we'd planned. I had a new job as well, working for a local branch of Lloyd's Bank. While Michael commuted up to the City each day, I settled into a slower, more suburban existence, and dreamed happily of the family we were about to create.

But it didn't happen. 1968 became 1969 and then, somehow, it was the seventies; 1970 passed and 1971. Though we couldn't have been happier with our lives and each other, I was becoming increasingly convinced that the events from my past were conspiring to deny me a second chance at motherhood. I was now twenty-eight years old and we'd been trying to have a baby for four years. Nothing had happened. I had yet to conceive.

As a consequence I was becoming more and more distressed. It seemed such a terrible waste for this to happen to us, and so unfair. I tried to be rational. These things *did* happen; they could happen to anyone. It was probably just random bad luck. But I couldn't help seeing it as a punishment, which felt so wrong. We weren't bad people. Did we deserve this? And even if I did, I'd paid my price, hadn't I? As a consequence, I felt angry and increasingly bitter about having to give up Paul. I also felt such guilt and such sadness for Michael. He'd taken me on, and I'd failed him.

By the spring of 1972, on advice from my doctor, Michael and I were being tested to see if they could work out the reason why we were having such difficulty conceiving. It seemed my whole life was now dominated by having one test or another, and then walking to the doctor's, as I was this morning, only to be told the next lot of bad news.

I was feeling particularly low, having been out at a function the night before with some close friends of ours, David and Joan. We'd married at the same time – David and Michael had been each other's best man – and Joan already had two little ones under three. She had been really upset, she'd confided tearfully when we were both in the ladies', on realising she might be pregnant for a third time. 'I can't bear it!' she'd cried. 'I really don't think I can bear it! If I am, I'm putting my head in the bloody gas oven!'

I'd said nothing, of course – or, rather, I made all the right noises – but now, with my GP, who was a kind and caring man, I couldn't seem to stop my tears from flowing. There had been yet another test, yet another frustratingly inconclusive result. If they couldn't work out why I wasn't getting pregnant, what hope, realistically, did Michael and I have?

But then my doctor shocked me. 'Angela,' he said gently. 'I've been thinking about your options. Have you and Michael thought about adoption at all?'

The question brought me up short, the word 'adoption' hitting me with a jolt. When you carry around a secret as big as mine, it makes you feel jittery any time anything to do with it is mentioned. What was he saying? Did he know something about me giving up Paul? I shook my head, braced for what he might be about to tell me. Of *course* he didn't mean that, I told myself. He couldn't. He meant *us* adopting, surely? He did.

'I have another patient,' he explained, 'a young girl who's pregnant – impossible circumstances, very sad, very difficult. She's only nineteen, you see. And the child's father is married. She has decided that she wants to give the child up to be adopted.' He paused, letting me digest this before continuing. 'And it occurred to me that, potentially at least, we have, in you and Michael, ideal adoptive parents. Which is why I thought I'd ask you if you wanted to discuss it with him, give it some thought.'

I nodded, trying to clear my head of all the thoughts and associations his words had unleashed. How cruel an irony that would be! Potentially we could end up adopting the child of a young girl who'd found herself in almost the same circumstances as I'd been in, while my own child – my flesh and blood – was lost to me. 'I don't know,' I said. 'It's such a lot to take in, such a lot to think about.'

I wondered, as I spoke, if he'd think and feel differently had he known about Paul. Perhaps not. He was such a decent man, so non-judgemental. But did this mean he held out no hope for us conceiving naturally? Was he already that sure we'd reached the end of the line?

'Not at all,' he reassured me. 'It's just another option to consider, as I say. And there's absolutely no rush to make a decision here. The baby isn't due until October. And you'll obviously need to go home and discuss it with Michael before we could even think about taking things further. It would have to be something you're both committed to, obviously.'

So I did go home and discuss it with Michael and, tentatively, we agreed that it might be the right thing to do. Heartbreaking as it was to face the reality of our situation, difficult as it was to accept the idea that the child would not be ours biologically, we both felt to miss this opportunity might condemn us to a lifetime of childlessness. Time was passing. We had to be realistic.

'And it's nurture not nature, remember,' my GP reassured us, having got us both back to discuss the matter further the following week. He'd just given us some more background – she was an office junior, and he was a coach driver – the implication being their lives were worlds away from ours. 'So you don't need to worry that the child won't *feel* like yours. It will.'

'I know that,' I said, a new idea forming in my mind. What did the couple who had adopted Paul think about *me*, in that respect? Did they take a view? Did they think ill of me for being the sort of girl who 'got into trouble'? Had Paul been a girl, might they have worried that she, too, had the potential for 'going off the rails'? It was such a grim thing to think. I felt a rush of sadness for this child's mother, and a powerful empathy for the horrible, life-changing, desperate thing she would soon do. It was impossible to detach myself from it.

'And you two will make such wonderful parents,' the doctor added warmly. 'I can't think of two people more perfect to adopt this baby, which I know matters to her greatly. She'll be so relieved to hear you've said yes.'

It was kind of him, but also so hard to hear.

I left the surgery that day with very mixed emotions. On the one hand I now had something tangible to hold on to. Our GP had explained that it was a straightforward process, and all we needed to do now was to engage a solicitor. Once the baby was born all the papers would be drawn up for the adoption process to take place straight away. Moreover, we'd have the child almost immediately after birth, so we'd would be in a position, as he pointed out, to bond with him or her in almost the same way a natural parent would.

On the other hand, I couldn't help feeling I was about to be a party to something that girl would have wished not to have happened. I tried not to dwell on it, but it was so hard. I kept thinking about the birth: what she was about to have to go through, and then the agony of immediately having to give her baby to us. Thank God for those eight weeks I'd had with Paul, I thought. Thank God I had the memory of them safely locked away.

The following few months were happy ones for me. I not only began to accept that I would not conceive naturally, but I also began to look forward to having the baby we both so wanted. But eight months into the girl's pregnancy, we were dealt another blow. My GP telephoned me at home one morning, and delivered the news himself.

'There's no easy way to say this, Angela,' he told me, 'so no preamble. The fact is that she's changed her mind. She's decided to keep her baby. I'm so sorry. I know this will be such a blow to you both.'

I cried and cried then, sitting at home alone, crying my heart out. To be so close and for this to happen felt like the cruellest of things. There was no one to blame here. It was just life, and we'd have to deal with it. And we persuaded ourselves it was all for the best. What else *could* we do? It wasn't meant to be, we agreed. It wasn't right. And it was surely best for the child that its mother was going to keep it. In my heart I admired her for her strength and determination, even though I couldn't help but envy her ability to make that choice. Yes, the world had changed since I'd had to part with Paul, thank God, but it was a brave decision and a hard road to travel nevertheless; although it was the early seventies, single mothers were still vilified. So how could I be anything but supportive of her courage?

As for ourselves, we'd have to put on a brave face and carry on. *Qué será, será*, as Michael had said all those years ago, even if it meant I was never to fall pregnant again. It certainly looked that way. Another year passed, another round of tests failed to uncover reasons. By 1974 I had come to accept the inevitable, when surgery for a tilted womb made me begin to wonder what damage my previous pregnancy and the birth might have done.

Shortly after that I gave up hoping. Another night, another function – this time with other friends, Jim and Jean. They were the only couple we knew who were still childless like us. My secret burned in me by now, a constant corrosive force in my life. I had had a child; I had voluntarily given him to others. Was that it, now? Had that been my one chance at motherhood? And what about Michael? He'd married me, accepting me and the past that came with me. When Jean announced her pregnancy that night I had to flee the room. Now it was me sitting in the ladies', sobbing my heart out.

My punishment, it seemed, must continue.

Chapter Sixteen

St Andrew's Catholic Church stands on the busy A28 Ashford Road, just a short walk from Tenterden's High Street and town centre. It's small, as churches go, and not particularly inspiring to look at, having been built post-war in a red-brick, utilitarian style. But like any church, it was a place of worship, of gentle light, of still air. Just entering St Andrew's always gave me a sense of peace, calm and comfort. Despite feeling that my faith had handed me such cruel justice, I could not give up on it.

So 1975 found me praying. I would regularly come here, though not for services; I never went to mass. The Catholic community was a small and close-knit one, and I didn't feel a part of it any more. I would just come to sit and pray, to have some quiet time.

Michael and I had recently returned from a holiday in Ireland. While we were there we'd spent some time staying with my cousin Mary, who was the loveliest, kindest and saintliest person I have ever known.

Mary knew about my difficulties conceiving, and spending time with her was good for my soul. But she also told me that if I prayed to St Anthony and Our Lady, she felt sure they would listen. I had no difficulty coming to this church and following her advice, not just because her own faith was so strong and persuasive, but also because, with everything physical and medical having been done now, I truly felt my only hope of getting pregnant again would be through divine intervention.

Cousin Mary didn't know about Paul, of course. So she didn't know how strongly I felt the weight of God's displeasure. But if God loved me, then surely He'd realise that I had atoned for my sins and was worthy of forgiveness by now?

My baby, my little Paul, would have been twelve. No, not *would* have been, *was* twelve. Twelve years old: a young boy on the cusp of adolescence. Was he tall or short? Was he big-boned or skinny? Was he sporty? Artistic? Full of confidence? Shy? I tried to imagine him, to visualise him in my mind's eye. Where did he live? What did he love? What were his favourite things now? How much did he know about where he came from? Who *I* was? Did he fret about it? Wonder about it? Think nothing of it? Did he ever pause to wonder where his lovely olive skin came from? Did he want to know the origins of that glorious head of hair?

But all my imaginings were just that – things I conjured up to keep him real for me. I knew nothing at all about him in the flesh, did I? No, that wasn't true. I *did*. I knew the blood that ran in his young veins was *my* blood. That the feet that kicked footballs, the legs and arms that hauled him up tree trunks, the hands that carefully formed the words he wrote in his schoolbooks, carried *me* with them, because they carried my genes. So what if my imaginings didn't quite match the reality? Those young limbs, that heart and soul, were connected to me.

These thoughts, and the attendant hurt, were for me only, however. On the outside, the lack of a child of our own notwithstanding, our lives were full and happy. Since giving up work to improve my chances of becoming pregnant, I had become a keen gardener and spent countless hours working on ours. I was also secretary of the local Conservative Association and an enthusiastic fundraiser and organiser of events. We had lovely friends, a full social life, lots of blessings to count, but there was still this huge void that I needed to fill.

I didn't want to replace Paul – I could *never* replace him – I just wanted to be a mother again. I wanted that so badly. I had all this maternal love inside me and nowhere to bestow it. How could God not see that and forgive me?

'Please,' I prayed. 'Please God. Let me have a baby. *Please* God. Haven't I paid my price now?'

By this time, Michael and I had begun an official adoption process with the local council. The law had changed, making private adoptions a thing of the past, and we had to go through a long complex series of interviews and screenings in order to be accepted as potential parents. It was a comfort to be moving forward, but despite my outward acceptance that this was to be our future, in my heart I simply couldn't give up hope that we might still have a child of our own.

I had plenty of things with which to occupy myself. We had moved again, to a house that was just around the corner; one we'd both fallen in love with long ago. It was another Georgian property – a real one this time – that stood in several acres, on a rise, at the top of a long drive. We would walk past it often, commenting on how forlorn it looked, and discuss all the things we'd do to make it lovely once again, should we be lucky enough to own it.

Naturally, when it came onto the market, we'd been to view it, only to find it was in an even worse state than we'd thought. But we'd seen beyond that and bought it, packed our belongings, leaving behind the bedrooms that had never seen babies, and set to work on our new home with vigour. It was an enormous project and, with Michael still working in the City, much of the hard manual work fell to me, but I didn't mind. If nothing else, at thirty-two I was still young, fit and able. Now we had a realistic hope of adopting a baby, I had a deadline to work to, and I was determined to meet it. If we were accepted as parents, I wanted our home to be ready.

And there, at least, my prayers *were* answered. In the spring of 1976, having been formally approved to adopt, we were told that the council had a baby for us that was due in November. I continued my renovations with renewed energy.

And then, in mid-April, I missed my period.

I'm going mad, I thought. I'm having a phantom pregnancy – that's what it is. It might sound ridiculous, but that the pregnancy could be real didn't once enter my head. After being unable to conceive for nearly a decade, it didn't seem possible.

Instead, I felt quite sure it was my body playing tricks. I was so convinced of this, after being obsessed with getting pregnant for such a long time, that I didn't say a word about it to Michael.

When I missed a second period, I was even more sure I was right: it was symptomatic of the extreme nature of my desire to have a child. I had read extensively on the subject, and I knew these things were relatively common. The mind could play all sorts of tricks on the body, and periods could stop for any number of reasons. It was to put my mind at rest, then, that I made an appointment with the doctor. My suspicions were confirmed: the pregnancy test I'd asked for came back negative.

The promised period did not appear, however. So I called the doctor again, because I was becoming anxious about having some sort of medical condition. If I wasn't pregnant – and I had just had it confirmed that I wasn't – then what exactly was happening to me?

'Give it a week,' he advised, seeming completely relaxed. 'Then come back and we'll do another test.'

I didn't tell him that I was being sick in the mornings, because I felt certain he'd start questioning my mental stability. I was worried that the authorities in charge of the adoption would have grave concerns if they thought I was unhinged. I waited the allotted week, then had another test, only this time, when I called to find out the result, I was told something I was convinced I'd never hear.

'Ah, Mrs Patrick,' the receptionist said gaily. 'The doctor

asked to speak to you himself. Just a moment, and I'll put you right through to him.'

I felt anxious then, despite her light tone. Perhaps something bad *was* happening to me. But when my doctor came on the line, his voice couldn't have sounded brighter either. 'Angela,' he said. 'I have wonderful news. I've got your results in front of me. You're pregnant!'

It took several seconds for this information to sink in. 'Are you absolutely sure?' I said, not quite able to believe it.

'Absolutely sure,' he confirmed. 'As I say, I have the piece of paper right here in my hand, and I can't tell you how pleased I am for you and Michael. Congratulations!'

Still I refused to believe him. 'For definite? I mean, there's no chance this could be a false positive?'

'Trust me,' he said. 'You are pregnant – around three months into it – so very definitely pregnant. Which means I'll need to see you sooner rather than later. Let me pop you back to my receptionist and she can get an appointment arranged for you. And, as I say, congratulations to you both!'

I put the phone down with shaking fingers. I had paint on them, I noticed, a constellation of white speckles, where I'd been using the roller in the living room. I could still hear *The Jimmy Young Show* burbling to itself on the transistor radio. I was *pregnant*. I had a baby growing inside me again.

And then I smiled, suddenly remembering the conversation Michael and I had had two days before. I'd been dressing. I was up early for something – I couldn't remember what now – and putting my bra on. 'You've grown!' he'd said, winking.

I sat down on the seat beside the hall table and placed my speckled hand over my tummy. There was nothing to see, nothing to feel, nothing to give me any clues to my condition other than the dispiriting sickness with which I'd been waking each morning and which now felt like the most wonderful thing in the world.

I did some sums then, counting on my fingers, back and forth, trying to work out all the whens, whys and wherefores of the calculation. The 20th of December, he'd told me. It would be due on the 20th of December. So when had this child been conceived, exactly? My brain couldn't seem to work it out. I stopped trying to remember. Did it even matter? Of course it didn't.

Instead I picked up the receiver again. It was 11.30. Michael would be on the floor of the Stock Exchange right now. But that was okay. The telephonist in his office, a couple of streets away, would answer the phone and transfer it straight through to the Hexagon. Michael worked in the gilt edge section, along with all the government brokers, who went on the floor in their traditional top hats. It made me smile to visualise him there, in the thick of it among them, and his reaction to what I was about to tell him. The phone rang six times before it was answered.

A baby, I kept thinking as I waited. A *baby*! It had actually happened. I couldn't stop grinning.

I felt a bit light-headed, almost tongue-tied, when I finally heard his voice. 'What are you doing around Christmas time?' I asked him. The background noise was deafening, so I had to speak up.

'I beg your pardon?' he said. 'What am *I* doing around Christmas time?' He sounded slightly short. It wasn't really on for him to take personal phone calls at work. I didn't care.

'Exactly!' I said brightly.

'How would *I* know? Um, whatever *you're* doing around Christmas time, I imagine. Angela, what—'

'Okay, so what are *we* doing around Christmas time?' I persisted.

'I don't *know*,' he said, displaying impressive patience at my nonsense. Or perhaps sensing my interrogation had some reason to it. 'You tell me,' he said. 'What *are* we doing, then?'

'Well, I don't know what *you're* doing, but I do know what *I'm* doing. I'm going to be having our baby!'

He had to phone me back. I'd said it at least three times, and we'd whooped and cried and laughed, and whooped some more, but he still had to phone me back five minutes later, because he was so shocked he hadn't fully taken it in.

'We're having a baby, definitely? I didn't dream that conversation?'

'We're having a baby,' I confirmed. 'Definitely.'

It took a couple more weeks for it to sink in properly for me too. In fact, I don't think I really allowed myself to believe I was pregnant, at least not till my early symptoms were joined by further evidence it was real. Once my waistline began to disappear and a little bump began forming, I finally accepted it and allowed myself to breathe out mentally.

There was still the question of the adoption. We realised

immediately that it would be very difficult to go ahead with it, as the baby we were adopting was due in late November, just a month before our own child was due to be born. So we waited till my doctor had unequivocally confirmed my pregnancy, and then pulled out of the process, still not quite believing we were having our own child. I think I pinched myself several times a day.

There was one other person for whom this long awaited pregnancy would, I knew, mean more than she could say, and that was my mother.

We decided it would be nice to go and tell her and Sam in person, so on a Saturday afternoon, a week or so after I'd seen the doctor, we drove up to Rayleigh, where they still lived in the same bungalow, to tell them both the wonderful news.

'I knew it,' she said, the second we'd arrived and the words had come tumbling out. 'I knew it!' And her expression was delightful to see. 'I could tell last time you were here,' she continued. We'd been up to visit a couple of weeks previously. 'You just had that look about you. I knew it!'

It had been a difficult few years for my mother, I think. I knew she had felt dreadful when I'd had to be admitted to hospital, once for the surgery on my womb and again after an awful reaction to tests on my fallopian tubes. I knew she felt my heartache at the endless disappointments keenly, as any mother would. I think she also carried a burden of guilt about Paul's adoption. How could she not? She'd had three children, I'd had just the one and I'd been made to give him up. I had not been allowed to mother him;

I was denied the opportunity to watch him grow. And with every passing year that I didn't conceive another child, I think she must have felt more and more guilty. Even if guilt wasn't her principal emotion, she was still my mother – how could she not feel my pain?

That said, she had also been positive throughout. It had taken seven years for her to conceive John after having Ray, so perhaps that had been her consolation. It might yet happen; one day it *would* happen. And now it had. On the day when we went up to tell her, I got a sense, albeit small, of how much she *did* care.

We'd gone into the kitchen, the two of us, to make a pot of tea and cut a sponge cake she'd made for our visit. She still had a look of such pleasure on her face. She was so visibly thrilled that she'd already noticed my condition, in that way only someone very close to you can. She'd never been demonstrative, and wasn't about to start now, but as she bustled around, pulling out a tray, fetching the sugar bowl and some spoons, she didn't need to be. The smile on her face said it all.

'You must take care of yourself now, Angela,' she said firmly. 'It's important that you don't overdo it. All that decorating you've been doing. You must slow down now you're expecting a baby. Angela, promise me you will.'

I said I would, of course, but I couldn't help wanting to point out just what gruelling physical labour we had all been forced to do in the convent, right up until our due dates. Had she any idea just how punishing it had been? How exhausted and demoralised and distressed we'd all felt? How much we could have done with just an ounce of compassion? A kind word, some support, a loving hug?

Would things have been any different if she *had* known all that? No, I thought, probably not. But I must be fair to her. She *hadn't* known, had she?

'I'm so happy for you, Angela,' she said then. '*So* happy.'

I believed her, and that was what mattered.

Chapter Seventeen

Our baby was born in the early hours of 19 December 1976 at Willsborough Hospital, in Ashford, where it had once again been decided that it would be prudent for me to be induced. The baby was due very close to Christmas, so with me being an 'older first-time mother' and staffing levels being an issue over the holiday period, they suggested it might be safer that way. I didn't argue. It was a long drive from home to the hospital and there was always a risk of being caught in heavy pre-Christmas traffic. So I'd packed a much smaller case with the things I would need for my short stay, including a change of nightwear for me, and a couple of all-in-ones for my new baby – all of it, this time, coming home with me.

It seems incredible today, but as far as I know, no one knew I'd already had a baby. To the antenatal and maternity staff – not to mention my GP – I was classed as an 'elderly primigravida', which apparently put me at risk of various complications, most of which didn't, in reality, apply.

'Look at you! You're a natural,' my midwife said, as my contractions began to strengthen. It was 6 p.m. on 18 December and the drugs they'd administered earlier that afternoon were definitely beginning to make their presence felt.

'You're doing so well!' agreed another nurse as I tried to breathe my way through them, being forcibly reminded that the memories I had of childbirth were nothing compared to the reality. She beamed encouragement, however, and smiled broadly as I grimaced. 'You've obviously listened at your antenatal classes, Angela!'

Oh, I thought, wincing, if only you knew.

It was odd having to keep up this pretence of ignorance during my labour, but it *was* all new and different this time. Whereas with Paul I'd felt wretched, alone and only tolerated by the staff, here I felt supported and optimistic. I was also relatively calm, knowing, at least in part, what was going to happen, and so much better able to deal with the pain. I knew what to expect now, both physically and mentally. This time I was also secure in the knowledge that when *this* baby was born, I would not have to endure the agony of giving it up.

If anything, what I'd mostly felt up to now was excited – a little scared, too, after the horrendous experience of my first birth. I'd read widely by this stage and had absorbed the mantra that held true in almost all cases: it would be easier – and faster – the second time around. But not that fast, particularly when your labour is started by induction. After dropping me at the maternity unit, and then bringing his parents to the hospital to say hello and good luck, Michael had gone home to grab some dinner.

'We'll call him,' the nurse had reassured me as he left. 'And in plenty of time, so don't worry. Better for him to go home and have a rest and a meal than hang around for hours. We'll have him back for the important bit, I promise.'

That had seemed fine while I was up on the ward, with its congenial atmosphere of calm expectation. But no sooner had I waved him off with a cheery 'See you later!' than it was time to get moving myself. I was transferred to the labour ward at seven in the evening, by which time the contractions had been growing steadily fiercer, and my recollections of Paul's birth similarly lucid. It *hurt*.

The new environment didn't help much either. The hospital was in a state of transition at that time, with the crumbling old one soon to be razed to its foundations to make way for a wonderful new facility up the road, which would be opening, with much flourish, in February. Sadly, I was sandwiched between these two events, and so was billeted, along with all the other unfortunately timed mothers, in a grim ward in a hospital that had once been a workhouse. Close to decommissioning, it was bare of all but the essentials, with the beds crammed in and only separated by curtains – there were none of the private rooms that are so common now.

The noise was deafening. Next to me, when I arrived, was a girl close to delivery, and her screaming and yelling scared me witless.

'Can you call my husband now?' I asked plaintively, my previous calm taking flight. 'Just to be sure he has enough time to get here?'

'Oh, he'll have time, my love,' my midwife reassured me,

albeit loudly, so I could hear her above the din. 'Baby won't be coming along for hours yet.'

So I lay there and tried to drown out the cacophony around me while I waited for Michael and the next contraction. Those 'hours yet' were going to be awfully long ones.

But, in the end, as often happens when you've lots going on, the time seemed to fly by. Michael arrived back, as promised, and took up his place by my bedside. No sooner had he done so than it was nearly midnight and I seemed to be approaching the point where the business of labouring might soon make way for the infinitely nicer prospect of having already given birth.

This time I was present: I was in pain but not delirious, frightened but with a clear idea of what I was frightened of and, with my husband at my side, able not to panic. The midwife, dashing frantically from bed to bed, popped her head around the curtain.

'I think it might be soon,' I gasped, ambushed by another wave of pain.

She shook her head. 'You've got a little way to go still,' she answered. 'Just breathe through them. That's the way. Just breathe through them.'

I was sucking on gas and air in great quantities now, floating up to the ceiling, then crashing back down to reality, and crushing Michael's hand every time.

'It's like Piccadilly Circus in here,' he observed drily. 'Is it always this busy?'

'How would *I* know?' I wailed back at him. 'Wahhhh . . .'

I'd lost all sense of time now, lost all focus on anything, except the way the contractions seemed to grip my whole body and squeeze every last breath from my lungs. And then something else. Something I remembered so clearly – the irrestistible, unstoppable, overwhelming need to push.

'Michael,' I hissed at him, removing the gas and air mouthpiece. 'You have to get the midwife! The baby's coming!'

I released his hand and he leapt up and shot through the curtains. I could hear him calling out, like an extra from a *Carry On* film. 'Nurse! We need a midwife! Where's the midwife! We need a midwife!' I would have smiled but my teeth were now clamped tight together. I knew the drill now. I must *not* push. I must stop myself from pushing. I couldn't recall why now, because I was dizzy with the need to, but I knew I must not – not till the nurse came. Thankfully, she was back in moments.

'Oh, my,' she declared, as she examined me. She sounded worried. 'I can see the head! Nurse!' she bellowed to someone else I couldn't see. 'We need to get Mrs Patrick to the delivery room – NOW!'

I couldn't have cared less which room I gave birth in. All I knew was that I was about to, whether I, or any of my baby manuals, liked it or not. Nevertheless, my bed and I were rushed out of the labour ward to the delivery suite, and less than ten minutes later our baby was with us. But then I realised not with *us*, just with *me*. I looked around, confused. Where was Michael?

'It's a girl! A baby girl!' the midwife told me, delightedly. 'And, goodness me – would you look at that mop of hair on her!'

Panting and dazed, I looked around for my husband, whom

I realised I'd not seen since he'd been running along beside me in the mad panic to get me where they wanted me. What had happened to him? Was he on the floor, having fainted? And then, just as I was about to ask, the door to the delivery room opened. 'Oh, Mr Patrick!' one of the nurses said, seeing him. 'I'm so sorry. Quick, come in. Come on in and meet your daughter!'

So he did, looking almost as dazed and confused as I was. 'They shut me out!' he protested. 'So I thought I wasn't allowed in!' Though there was no annoyance in his voice as he looked at our baby, just an expression of profound relief. By now they'd cut the cord and she was nestled against my chest. He stood and gazed in apparent wonder at this new life we'd created. Then he looked back at me. 'Good Lord,' he said, grinning now. 'She looks like she's done ten rounds with Henry Cooper!'

As he was to confess to me only a couple of days later, it would be 2.30 in the morning before it really sank in for him. While he was driving home to bed along deserted streets, Christmas lights twinkling everywhere, Johnny Mathis came on the radio singing 'A Child Is Born'. Michael cried the rest of the way home.

We'd had no preference, of course. All we wanted was a healthy child, but when our baby was born I was secretly so glad we'd been blessed with a daughter. I would have loved a son equally, but there was always this nagging sense that, for me, a boy might feel like a replacement for Paul, who was now in my mind every moment. We named her Katharine, and I was shocked at how much like her brother she looked, from the tone of her skin to her cute little features to that same unruly thatch of black hair; both were born on a Sunday, both Sagittarians. I cherished all these points of connection.

I stayed in hospital for five days, and how different those days were to those I'd spent in the lying-in room at Loreto Convent. Swamped with presents and visitors, and love and attention, I felt wrapped in a warm bubble of love and gratitude. Here I could properly care for my baby. I could cuddle her at any time I wanted, I could put her to my breast and feed her, I could pick her up and soothe her when she cried. As the roof in the soon-to-be-demolished nursery was leaking, I had her by my side every minute of every day. Some things were similar – the exhaustion, the sore boobs, the painful stitches – but the experience of having her couldn't have been more different. Despite my great joy, it made my heart ache for my little boy, now thirteen years old, for whom this wonderful start in life had been denied.

As I write, the early days of Katharine's life are now the blur of fond memories that such a joyous experience should be. I remember those first precious days of just me, her and Michael, and how we tucked ourselves away, shunning the usual round of Christmas trips and visitors, in order that we could get to know our daughter better.

I remember Boxing Day, and being so keen to sit down and watch *Oliver!*, and waking up just as the closing credits rolled. I recall her little nursery, which we'd decorated together for her: the wallpaper dotted with red bunnies, the matching curtains, the Italian cot, the cream carpet (so impractical but at the same time so perfect), the tiny clothes, the white cot bumper, the little mobile.

I recall the presents, including the twenty-three dresses we were sent as gifts for her. It astonished me, the kindness of people I barely knew. Even the waitress in the restaurant where Michael sometimes had lunch bought Katharine a present – a pink teddy bear, which she still has today.

I remember our lovely pram – solidly coach built and so stately – and how thrilling it was to go out and push it around Tenterden after so many years of seeing other mothers with other prams, and trying to quell the feeling of desperate longing. I remember how good it felt, now I'd swapped baby-bump for baby, when people wanted to peek in and say hello to our daughter, and I was finally allowed to be a proud mum.

I particularly recall driving up to Essex to visit my mother and stepfather, and how genuinely thrilled they were to see us. My mother was sixty-nine now, Sam seventy-two, and I knew how much it meant to her to see me happy.

And I *was* happy now – the happiest I'd been in such a long time. I often wondered: did this mean that God had forgiven me at long last? It certainly felt that, in giving me this perfect baby daughter, He had decided to give me a second chance. But had He forgiven me sufficiently to answer my prayers? Would He reunite me with her brother one day? I wanted that so very much, but I could only hope and wait.

And I did wait – for the next seventeen years.

PART THREE

Chapter Eighteen

19 January 1994

I didn't know anything about it until much later in the day, but there was something about the letter that dropped on the doormat that morning which stopped Michael dead in his tracks. I was still in bed. He liked to enjoy a quiet five minutes with his newspaper on weekday mornings, so we'd evolved a routine before going to our respective jobs: he'd bring me up cereal, toast and tea, and one of the newspapers, then return downstairs to eat his own breakfast in the kitchen with the other.

He'd just brought mine up when the postman arrived, and reached the hall as the letter slid through the letterbox. He didn't know why, but as soon as he saw the unfamiliar handwriting he had a powerful sense of what it might be about. He turned around then, and made his way back up the stairs, brought it to me and left the bedroom.

Thirty years is a very long time by anyone's yardstick, so lacking my husband's impressive intuitive powers, I had no such inkling about what I now held in my hands. Not straight away, anyway. I had never given up hope that Paul might one day try to find me. On his twenty-first birthday I'd even gone back to St Andrew's church. I'd prayed so hard that day that he might find me. But once that birthday was behind us, my hope had begun to fade. It was still there, but with each passing year it lessened. Had he wanted to find me, surely by now he *would* have found me? I knew the law had changed to make the process easier for adopted children; they could now have access to their adoption files. Though knowing that had initially filled me with hope, as the years following the legislation had passed without contact, it actually made it harder. I could no longer tell myself that he was trying to find me but couldn't.

Now here in my hands was this ordinary letter: this letter with its unfamiliar handwriting, its London postmark and its air of mystery. I put my tray carefully to one side on the duvet, turned the letter over and slipped my finger under the envelope's flap. I'm not even sure what I might have been thinking as I did this, because every detail of those moments is gone now. They were all swept away in the instant I pulled out the single page inside, opened it out flat and saw the address. For, neatly handwritten in the top right-hand corner, I read the words *73 St Charles Square, London W10.*

People talk lots about hearts skipping beats, don't they? Or breath being taken away, worlds tilting on their axes, sudden pyrotechnics exploding in the sky . . . I don't doubt that, for some, there are moments like these. But I can't adequately describe the emotion that overcame me when I saw that address.

I read on:

Dear Mrs Patrick,
I have been trying to find an old friend of mine, Angela
Brown, who used to live in Rayleigh, Essex, and my
search has led me to you, so I do hope I've found the right
Angela!
   I was Frances Whiteley when we first met in Epping in
1963, and of course we had another friend, Paul, whom
I'm sure you remember . . .

I cried out then, involuntarily. I let out a howl of such magnitude that, seconds later, I could hear Michael bounding back up the stairs.

I have recently met Paul again, and I thought it would be a
nice idea for us all to get together again for a reunion. I
know it's a long time ago and we've all moved on, but hope
you'll at least give me a ring and let me know how you are,
even if you don't wish to meet us again.
Best wishes,
Frances Holmes

The paper trembled in my hand now, so I steadied it with my other one. By the time Michael appeared in the doorway – in a matter of seconds – I had homed in on three of those neatly penned phrases, and rereading them caused tears to spring to my eyes. *All moved on . . . hope you'll at least . . . even if you don't wish to meet us . . .* They swam before me, all of them such perfectly formed letters, all of them joined to create perfectly formed words, all of them gently yet earnestly entreating that I would at least consider the possibility of getting in touch.

I was now sobbing uncontrollably, as thoughts began to clamour, as I imagined the journey Paul must have made to get to this point. Just how much had it taken for this letter to reach my hands? It had been so long now – he would be thirty – how hard must it have been for him to make this decision?

To think that he might be waiting somewhere, braced for my rejection, broke my heart. If I could have been granted one wish at that moment it would have been that I could be immediately spirited to wherever he was, so I could hold him tight, and tell him, that no, no, no, *no*! He need not worry for an instant longer. He needn't doubt he'd done the right thing. That I had *not* moved on, ever. That he *didn't* need to hope. That I *did* wish – oh, God, I could not have wished harder! For it was so painful, in that instant of rereading, to know somewhere out there my child was suffering the agony of not knowing. That he'd searched for me, and found me – though did he even know he *had* yet? No, he didn't. Because he had to wait some more, didn't he? For me to get the message back to him that I *was* here and that I loved him and that I had never once stopped loving him. That he need never wonder how much ever again.

Still unable to speak for sobbing, having read and reread the letter, I passed it over to Michael. He read through it silently before coming to sit beside me on the bed, putting his arm around me and holding me close.

'Hmm, I was right then,' he said quietly.

*

Michael counselled, wisely – more than once that day – that I must try not to get overexcited. There were so many potential potholes down this road I was about to travel, and he was anxious that I set off forewarned. This man – my lost son – was going to be an unknown quantity, a stranger. Suppose we didn't click? Suppose we didn't warm to each other? Suppose the issues he might have about being given up for adoption were so great that we couldn't get beyond them? There was, Michael also pointed out, every possibility that his curiosity, once satisfied, would abate. How would I feel if, now he'd tracked me down and knew where he came from, he didn't want any further communication? But no amount of wise counsel, however important it was that I absorb it, could stop my brain from fizzing with questions.

'Oh, what will he look like?' I wondered both aloud and in my head. 'What will he sound like? What will he *be* like?' Would he be studious? Gregarious? Shy? A jack-the-lad type? Would he wear glasses? Would he be short? Would he be tall? I was so consumed by excitement that I could hardly keep still, and though I kept trying to temper it, and heed Michael's cautions, I honestly can't imagine ever feeling such an intense level of emotion or excitement again.

'This is the most wonderful news I could have possibly received ever,' I told Frances Holmes when I was finally able to call her that lunchtime. I had been trying hard to concentrate on my job at the Town Hall all morning, but had to keep disappearing into the ladies' loo at regular intervals; I just kept welling up with tears, overcome. I couldn't seem to stop it, and the clock couldn't creep round to 1.00 soon enough. When I got home I was like a woman possessed. I flew through the front door, hustled our golden retriever, Monty, out through the back into the garden, pulled off my coat and dumped it, even as I rushed to the phone.

There was a pause now – quite a long one. 'Really?' she said.

'Of course!' I responded, shocked. 'How could it *not* be?'

Her tone was measured. 'Then you're very unusual.'

'Unusual?' I was even more shocked. 'Why?'

'Because that's not the response I usually get,' she explained. 'That is, if I get one at all. It might seem impossible to imagine but, you know, something like ninety-eight per cent of all the birth mothers I'm asked to write to don't wish to be contacted by their child.'

I was stunned to hear this. It had been such an ache in me, such a yearning, for three decades. It seemed unfathomable. 'You're right,' I said. 'I do find that impossible to imagine.' I thought back to all the girls who had suffered the agony of loss with me. Would that apply to them? I couldn't conceive of it. And yet . . .

'There are a myriad reasons, of course,' Frances continued. 'But in many cases, perhaps the vast majority of cases, it's an event in their past that they've kept secret ever since. So it becomes complicated; potentially destructive to the relationships and families they've built since.'

I got the feeling she must have had this conversation many times in the years since I'd last seen her. Then I thought again of all those girls who had told no one, who'd travelled to the convent in secret, too terrified to tell a soul. How terrible it must be, then, to have their lost child make contact and feel unable to acknowledge their existence.

'But anyway,' Frances continued. 'Let's talk about you. You'll be wanting to hear about James, won't you? He's a policeman, you know, which is what helped him trace you ...'

It took a moment for this to sink in. Michael's earlier words of caution now had some resonance for me. It had been Paul in my thoughts and heart these last thirty years. That he was called James was upsetting, a jerk back to the reality of a person unknown and a life lived without me. He was a stranger, just as Michael had said. But I put that to one side. When we met, it would be different. When I saw him, I just knew, I'd see myself.

'So what happens now?' I asked Frances. 'Should I write to him? Phone him?'

'No, not yet,' she said. 'The next step is for me to go back to him, convey the details of our conversation – and I know he'll be so pleased – and invite him to write directly to you, though via this office. I normally suggest that they enclose a photo or two with the letter, and perhaps some idea of when and how you could meet up. That can even be here, if you like. That's what some people do. And let's hope it won't be too long,' she finished. 'Though given you're so pleased to hear from him – which is lovely, Angela, I truly am so pleased for you both – it's going to seem it, I'm quite sure!'

I nearly blurted out '*And tell him how much I love him*!' but then I thought again of Michael. This was a time to be calm, to temper my excitement. I must try, and try *hard*, not to get my hopes up too much.

As I put the phone down, memories of that day at the Crusade of Rescue came flooding back, assaulting my senses and making me cry all over again. They were tears of relief this time, but also a metaphorical deep breath. I had not been able to say goodbye to my infant son that afternoon, and the pain of that loss had never left me. I had waited thirty years to tell him how much I loved him. I could manage to wait a few more days.

If I could wait, though only just, to speak to my son, I was desperate to tell my daughter right away.

'I don't think you should tell her. I really don't. Not yet.'

It was the evening now, and Michael was speaking. Once dinner had been cleared, and Katharine was busy upstairs revising for her A levels, we'd gone out to take Monty for a walk. It was a job that on most days Michael tended to do alone, but we needed a chance to talk privately and this seemed the most logical way to do that.

'You don't? But surely I must?' I said, surprised. 'I don't think I can bear to hide it from her. It feels wrong to exclude her. I feel like I'm going to burst as it is.'

Michael squeezed my hand. 'But sweetheart, you *have* to. At least till you've made contact. It's an awful lot for you to expect her to take in, whatever happens, but suppose it doesn't work out? Suppose it all comes to nothing—'

'That's not going to happen. I just can't see that – not from what Frances said, I really can't, Michael. She *has* met him, remember. And she said he would be so pleased to hear that I was—'

'But it still *might*,' he persisted, gently but firmly pushing his point home. 'You *haven't* met him yet, remember. You can't know. You can't read his mind, can you? For all you know, he might have no interest in having a relationship with us [I was so touched by that 'us']. How do we know it's not just that he's going to have a baby or something, and wants to find out a little more about his genes? How do you know – and I'm not trying to seem negative, I'm really not, just playing devil's advocate – that he hasn't already got a child, say, and that there's some sort of hereditary medical problem, something that he wants to find out about? Suppose it's something like that?'

'Well, if that's the case, then, well, it doesn't preclude us also trying to—'

'I'm not saying it *does*.' He stopped on the path while Monty investigated a tree. 'Look, poppet,' he said. 'All I'm asking is that we wait. Just until you've heard from him. Just until you know a little more about him. I think that, what with her exams so close and everything, it would be better to be sure what we're dealing with than to land her with this bombshell and then have it come to nothing. I mean, look how painful it's been for you, knowing he's been out there but not knowing anything about him. Can you imagine how big a thing it would be for Kate? To know she has a brother and then have the exact same thing happen?'

I nodded. He was making perfect sense, as always. And his words were spot on. Our daughter had always hankered after an older brother. Not a little sister or brother – which, sadly, had never and was never going to happen – but an older brother. That had always been her wish when she was smaller: to have a big brother like several of her friends had. So, yes, it would mean such a lot to her. Michael was right. I shouldn't tell her, not till I was absolutely sure that Paul – James – really *did* want to know her. And yet . . .

'Look,' Michael said, as we walked on. 'It just seems the safest thing to do. If it does come to nothing – and, God, I so hope it doesn't, you *know* that – then surely it's best that things remain as they are? There's no point in her knowing if she doesn't need to.'

And he *was* right. I knew that. Why burden her with it? It made so much more sense to wait a bit and see what happened. Oh, but it was going to be *so* hard.

Chapter Nineteen

I was half demented with anxiety.

For the next two weeks I lived in a kind of personal hell, preoccupied, stuck in this horrible limbo of knowing he was out there and had taken that life-changing first step. Not knowing what would happen next, and having been so bombarded with them by Michael, my mind couldn't help but keep focusing on all the negatives. All those cautionary comments he'd made, and which I'd tried to ignore, were now lining up to make themselves clear to me. It had been sane and sensible of Michael to prepare me for the worst, but as a result, Paul – no, James – had become this unknowable power in whose hands rested so much of my future happiness.

Would he change his mind about wanting to meet me now? Having satisfied himself that he now knew where and who I was, would his curiosity have been satisfied after all? Would he have had second thoughts about the emotional can of worms he might open? Might he have now told his adoptive parents that he had found me and, having done so, been faced with a reaction so powerful that he decided that to pursue it would be too painful for them?

Fretting was pointless. I could do nothing about any of it, could I? He knew who and where I was. I still knew nothing about him, bar the scraps of information Frances Holmes had given me. If he decided not to follow through – for whatever reason I could conjure, be it crazy or rational – that *would* be the end of it. There would be nothing I could do.

So I kept trying to carry on – go to work, eat, sleep, function normally, *appear* normal – shored up by blind optimism and Michael's steadying presence. Though he counselled me not to get carried away, in one thing he was confident: my son would be in touch. 'He will be,' he kept telling me, as each day went by without a letter. Perhaps he was worried that he'd sent me spinning too far the other way. 'Stop worrying, sweetheart. He *will*,' he kept saying. 'He wouldn't have come this far if he didn't mean to see it through. You must know that?'

I knew that. But still I fretted, and not only about myself; I also fretted about Katharine. It was becoming increasingly difficult not to tell her what was happening, as I was well aware I wasn't myself. I was jittery, preoccupied and overemotional, and I was finding the burden of the secret hard to cope with. No, I'd not told her about Paul – there'd never been any point because there'd never have been a benefit. But now that my secret ache had become flesh and blood – *her* flesh and blood – it felt all wrong, morally wrong, to keep it from her.

She knew there was something going on, though. It had been unusually warm and balmy for early February that year, almost springlike, and I'd taken to spending periods lying on the hammock in our garden. It was one of those big swing seats, more like a swinging sofa, really. It had a big overhanging canopy and canvas side panels, which kept the cold out, and it had a wonderful view of the orchards and woods beyond the garden.

I was lying there one afternoon, trying and failing to read a book, when having returned home from school early, she came out and found me. She was in her uniform but she had her own distinct style. She had long hair, very thick, which she rarely tied back, and though she'd gone through a slightly alarming 'grunge' stage at fifteen, she was beginning to change into an elegant young woman. She wasn't a follower, either, preferring to go her own way. While everyone else seemed obsessed with Oasis and Robbie Williams, Katharine would be listening to PJ Harvey. She plopped herself down on the seat beside me, and began to swing it back and forth.

'Hello, darling,' I said, as she leaned across to kiss me. 'Good day at school?'

'All right,' she said. 'Same as yesterday, pretty much.' Then she turned. 'Mummy?' she then asked. 'Are you okay?'

I began swinging the seat with her. 'Yes, I'm fine,' I said.

'Are you sure? Only I was wondering. Has somebody upset you?'

I shook my head, conscious of how closely I was being scrutinised. 'No, no,' I said. 'Not at all, no, everything's fine. Busy at work, of course. A bit tired, but no, honestly, I'm fine.'

'Only you don't seem yourself,' she persisted. 'So I wondered if, you know, there was something that's upset you.'

I racked my brains for something I could make up that would be sufficiently plausible to put her mind at rest, and came up with nothing. Oh, this was killing me. I so wanted to blurt it all out.

'Honestly,' I said again. 'I'm *fine*.' She didn't look convinced and I hated myself for deceiving her. We'd always been so close. *Were* so close. And then I hit upon something that *was* true. 'Though you know what?' I took her hand. 'I *am* fretting. Just a little. About your exchange trip to France.' She was going to Lyon in a couple of weeks, as part of her A-level course, French being one of the subjects she was studying. 'Feels like such a long time, ten days,' I said. 'And you'll be so far away.' I stood up, pulling her with me. 'And I'm going to be worrying about you.' I would be too. I'd be just like this while she was away. I always was. 'I know I'm just being silly,' I said, as we headed up the garden. 'But you know what I'm like. Come on, let's go in and have a cup of tea, shall we?'

'Honestly, Mummy,' she said, apparently satisfied. 'I'm seventeen!'

And then, finally, the torture was over. On 3 February, another letter dropped on the mat. I arrived home from work and there it was, waiting for me, presumably having come in the second post.

It was a bigger envelope this time, brown manila and type-written, and when I picked it up I could tell there were lots of pages in it. I couldn't stop myself. I ripped it open and pulled out the contents.

Inside was a short letter, which was once again from Frances, telling me that she had now enclosed a letter from James, and that she also had his address and phone number on file, so that if I wanted to I could now contact him directly. She also told me that I should not hesitate to contact her, in any case, if there was anything I wanted to discuss, or if I was worried about any difficulties that might arise, particularly in regard to telling Katharine.

I paused, put that letter down and scrutinised the other – a second envelope, cream this time, not brown, with just the word 'Angela' handwritten on it. I felt the bulk of the letter in my hand. It was so *fat*. Just knowing that made my body flood and tingle with adrenalin. It was fat in that way that letters used to be in my childhood, in the days of pen pals, long missives and Basildon Bond.

Now I did take my time, even though my fingers were already trying to get the better of me again. I put the letters down on the hall table, along with the other post, a couple of bills, carefully nudging aside the vase of flowers and telephone that both sat there. I then took off my coat, hung it on the newel post, replaced my door keys in my handbag and then, swinging the bag back onto my shoulder, picked up the single cream envelope and took it into the kitchen.

Monty was waiting for me, as he always was, tail wagging furiously, so I put the letter down on the table and made a big fuss of him for five minutes, before unlocking the utility room door so he could go outside. I then made myself a cup of tea, pulled out a chair from under the table, sat down, took a sip and picked up the envelope again.

I took my time opening it, not wanting to rip something so precious, and pulled out a letter and two photos. It was the photos that I attended to first. I pulled them out – they were face down – and slowly turned them over, revealing first a picture of a man who no person, however persuasive, however adamant, however definite, could *ever* have convinced me wasn't my son. I could see Peter, if only fleetingly, in the shape of the head and the angles of his face, but the likeness between the two of us was so arresting it made me gasp out loud. Oh, God – here he was! My baby! He was real at long last! All those years of imagining what he might look like, and here he was. I could hardly believe my own eyes.

I had wanted so, so much for him to bear evidence of me. And he did, he so gloriously did. He looked very much like me, like my brother Ray, so much one of us, so like Katharine – how much, I couldn't wait to show her! Everything about him was very obviously like us: the height – he looked so tall! – the olive skin, the smile, the dense black hair … It was so strong, this family resemblance, that it made the back of my neck prickle. Here he was, the grown-up version of that tiny baby I'd had to part with. If I'd been overcome in the aftermath of reading Frances's first letter, it was as nothing to the wash of emotion I was drowning in now.

The other photo was of him again, this time with an attractive young woman: his wife, perhaps, or an adoptive sister? It was hard to say, but they looked close. But I would find out who she was, I realised; it would all be in his letter. I propped the photos by my mug. Now I could devour the letter, which I did.

It was the Cambridgeshire address that caught my eye first. Cambridgeshire, I thought with a jolt – such a long way away.

But then I scolded myself. I should be grateful. It wasn't *that* far. I was lucky. He could have lived anywhere, couldn't he? The North of England, Europe, Australia even. But instead it was Cambridgeshire – *not* so very far.

My eye travelled a little further down. The letter was pleasingly thick in my hands, running to several closely written pages. As with a novel you start reading and immediately fall in love with, I didn't want to leap ahead and spoil the ending. So I didn't flick through it, or count the pages. I didn't wish to know. I just unfolded the letter, as I had done with the ones from Frances, and gazed upon it, this letter from my son.

His writing made me start, it was so lovely to look at: such elegant handwriting, gently right-sloping cursive, the tails of the tailed letters all finished with a uniform loop, lending it an air of such grace. It was silly to dwell on style over substance, perhaps, but I felt like you do when you see anything that is decorative and also very meaningful – a wedding cake, say, or the structure of an important molecule, something beautiful to feast your eyes on as well as your other senses, or like a holiday, perhaps. Some of the pleasure of a holiday, surely, is the sense of anticipation you get from poring over pictures in a brochure, and the promise of the reality to come?

Most of all, I felt an overwhelming sense of maternal love. How could there not be, knowing that these words had been written by my child? Was it any wonder I wanted to savour them carefully? They were the first steps towards knowing the man he had become.

I gripped the letter in both hands and began to read.

Dear Angela,

Since speaking with Mrs Holmes late last week, I have been looking forward to writing this letter, but have been unsure what to write and so perhaps this might arrive later than I would have liked.

I have decided to write openly, as my feelings dictate, so I apologise if the letter appears disjointed. It seems strange to be writing to you after all these years, although I must say I have often thought about you, hoping you were okay and that you were settled and had a family of your own.

My mother and father had explained to me as long ago as I can remember that I was adopted, telling me that my 'real' mother wasn't, for whatever reason, allowed or able to keep me and had therefore put me up for adoption. I knew your name was Angela Brown and that you had named me Paul — my name incidentally is James Paul — that I had been born in Epping and that you were a translator and were tall, dark and attractive.

My parents loved me more than I can say, and my sister Vicky was also adopted through the Crusade of Rescue. I even had 'my special day', so did my sister, like a second birthday, which in fact was the day my parents collected me from the Crusade of Rescue.

As a small child I was very happy and my thoughts never really strayed to my past until my birthday, when my parents at a private minute of the day would say 'I bet someone else is thinking about you' (in a nice way, that is).

Then I would think about you and hope as I do now that you spared me some thoughts.

It wasn't until I was older, in my early teens, that I thought about you more and sometimes I resented what had happened to me, particularly as one does as a teenager, having fallen out with my parents at that time. I used to resent you, thinking the worst, and this, I think, made me put thoughts of you out of my head, except, of course, on my birthday.

By this time the law had been passed to allow adopted children access to their natural parents and when suggested by my parents I was adamant I was happy not knowing.

As a child I even looked like my father in that I am slim-medium build, dark and tall, but now and for some years I have had a 'swarthy' complexion. The rest of my family look typically English and I have often wondered if there is any foreign blood in me.

People have always, as a result, taken me to be Spanish or Italian or have family ties as such, and I have always played along with it, although I look nothing like my family.

It has taken me thirty years to decide to find out the real truth.

Although in my youth I was rebellious and felt resentful towards you, I have now grown up mentally and for a number of years have wondered what has become of you.

I have had great curiosity to find out what you look like, whether I'm like you, whether you are well and are okay or may need my help in any way. I even feel something for you, and yet I don't even know you.

I am so glad I have eventually done this. I am a very confident person but for years there has always been a little insecurity surrounding me and I think this stems from not really knowing who I am or where I come from.

I have always prayed you are okay and have not come to any harm. To hear you are married and have a daughter is fantastic news for me. I am pleased, as it puts my mind at rest.

It has been good to hear more about you through Mrs Holmes, where you came from, etc. I never thought my mother was an Essex Girl! I have racked my brains trying to work out what a code translator was.

On the forms Mrs Holmes has, it appears you have blue eyes and dark hair. It still hasn't taken me any further forward as to my tanned appearance, so I must have to put that down to my father.

When I revisited the Crusade, or Catholic Children's Society, as it is now, I found the information on the forms fascinating but upsetting. It made things seem very real. I was particularly touched, and visibly upset by a letter I was shown, written by you, asking if my name Paul had been kept. As you know now, it has.

The letter made me accept more easily that you had cared and didn't really want to let me go, contrary to thoughts I had had as a teenager.

I must tell you now, I meant to at the beginning, that

under no circumstances have I intended to put pressure on you and I certainly don't want to interfere in your new life. That is not my intention. I just want you to know now, as I do feel for you.

When Mrs Holmes told me you had replied to her letter I was ecstatic, and hearing her tell of your reaction was great; apparently the response is not always as good. I'm lucky and I thank you.

You may know already that I am a policeman; my work now is based in special operations, drugs and serious crime. It is funny: when I joined the police force, I did my initial training at Ashford. I wonder, did you live in Tenterden then?

I have my own house near Cambridge, where I live with my fiancée, Karen, who I have known for a few years. She is gorgeous and we are the best of friends. She has supported me while I have decided to contact you – she accompanied me to the Crusade and has encouraged me.

We are to be married in Wales, where her parents come from, which I really look forward to.

I have enclosed a photograph of the both of us. Perhaps you will meet her soon – I would like that. I know she would, and I hope it is soon.

I am signing off now because I would like to tell you more about myself but in person. I really hope we can meet soon. I look forward to it. I enclose my telephone number, pager number and you have my address. Perhaps you could write, or contact Mrs Holmes and leave a contact number

for me. Or arrange a date with Mrs Holmes, if you would
like to meet me. I would prefer not to go to the Crusade of
Rescue, please.

   Please make contact.
   Yours sincerely,
   James x

I put the letter down. Then I picked it up again and reread it from
the beginning. I must have read it a dozen times – perhaps more –
by the time Michael came home at 6.30. In fact, I can no longer
recall any detail of that afternoon, apart from sitting there at the
kitchen table, reading the letter over and over again.

'I must tell Kate now,' I said to Michael, once he too had sat
down and read James's letter. He had been stunned by how
much James looked like both of us, and I knew he could see
how much I wanted to share this with her. But, perhaps thankfully, she had come home from school at the same time as he
had – he'd picked her up from the station on his way – and had
immediately gone upstairs to change out of her uniform and
make a start on her homework. I also knew it wouldn't have
been fair to Michael, having agreed that I'd wait, to have presented him with a fait accompli when he walked in, if she'd
come in earlier.

He was very insistent that I didn't tell her – not yet. He shook
his head. 'Please just meet him first, sweetheart. Please let's not
involve Kate until you've done that, at least. We know how you
feel, and it seems clear from his letter that he's keen to get to
know you, but until you speak face to face you have no idea

what's going to happen next. He might care about you – I'm sure he does – but that doesn't necessarily mean he wants you – us – in his life.'

I knew where Michael was coming from. I knew it was important he protect his daughter. But I felt strongly – even more so, having read James's letter, that he *did* want us in his life. If anything, it felt as though his principal worry was that he wouldn't be welcome in *ours*. *Please make contact*, he'd written. How much clearer could that have been? 'But he's already said he'd like us to meet his fiancée,' I pointed out.

Michael nodded. 'I know that, and I'm sure that's what he does want. But there are other people in this equation, don't forget – his adoptive parents. He might want all sorts of things, but, in the end, find it too difficult – too hurtful to them, too many divided loyalties. After all, can you imagine how all this might be for them?'

I had thought of them, and just as it had been my dream that this day would come, for them, perhaps, it had been the opposite. They would not wish for the day when it wouldn't seem enough that they were his parents. I knew how much *I'd* thought about that when we'd decided to adopt a child. This would be hard for them, all of it. I knew that. I said so.

'Exactly,' Michael said. 'So this will be new territory for his family, too. Which is why I think you should leave it till after you've actually met him to tell Kate. I know it's hard, but just so you know you can be sure. It's only a matter of days, that's all.'

'I know, but—'

'And you could perhaps try to arrange to meet him while

Kate's away in Lyon on her school trip. That will give you a few days to play with, won't it? And you can tell her the wonderful news the minute she gets home.'

I wanted to argue my point further, because by now I was desperate to tell her, but was I being selfish, careering about in my giddy whirlwind of excitement, not thinking straight? I must be fair to Michael, I realised, and respect his views too. So I agreed. We would wait until I'd met him.

Chapter Twenty

Now it was time for me to sit down and write, to reply to James's letter, and so begin the process of getting to know each other, but try as I might, each beginning seemed to founder. There was so much to say, and I couldn't get the words right. I kept starting, and then abandoning it, and then starting again.

'I can't do this!' I wailed to myself, sitting amid the detritus of my many false starts at the kitchen table, an envelope and the three photographs I'd selected to go with my letter sitting in neat pile in the middle of it all, waiting. But I couldn't seem to find the right way to say what I wanted to. Knowing how much I'd pored over James's every word to me, it really mattered that I get it right. Perhaps that was the problem. Perhaps I shouldn't even try. There was too much to say, and too much emotion involved. Maybe I should abandon trying to commit my heart to paper, and wait until I could tell him how I felt face to face.

Dear James,
It was so wonderful to receive your lovely letter. I have read
it at least a hundred times just to reassure myself that it

isn't all a dream. I can't begin to tell you how happy I am that you have contacted me.

After several attempts at a reply, I find it impossible to relate in a letter the events of the past and the circumstances of your birth. That time was for me a very sad, lonely and unhappy one, and full of painful memories that I have kept buried deep inside me. To try and explain in a letter, with the depth of emotion involved, is impossible, and I think would be best left till we meet. For that reason I have decided to write only of my life as it is at present. I hope you can understand.

I have been married to Michael for twenty-seven years. He is a wonderfully kind, considerate and thoughtful person. He has made me very happy and is thrilled that we are to be reunited. We have lived in Tenterden since 1968 and moved to our present house almost a year ago.

We have a daughter, Katharine (Kate to us). She is seventeen and, although a stroppy teenager at times, is generally a very caring and sensitive young lady. She is not unlike you, as you can see from the photograph of her. She is still at school studying for her A levels in French, Russian and Spanish. She speaks Spanish like a native and looks very much like one too.

Both Michael and I now work in Tenterden. Michael is a financial consultant and investment manager with a firm of solicitors. I am assistant town clerk with the town council, working in the town hall every morning.

I have two brothers: Raymond, a very youthful sixty-

one, and John, who is fifty-four. They are both married
with children and grandchildren too numerous to mention
now.

Thank you for sending the photographs. You and Karen
look a gorgeous couple. I am so pleased to hear that you are
happy and that you are to be married soon. I am glad she
has supported you while you were trying to contact me. I am
so looking forward to meeting her.

There is such a lot for me to tell you but little of it
would be appropriate in a letter except to say that you were
right in thinking I did care about you, so very much.

I can't wait to meet you and, like you, would prefer not
to go to the Crusade of Rescue. I think we will have to
speak together on the telephone to arrange a time and place.
Because of your work, it might be easier for you to ring me,
perhaps at home on any weekday between 2 and 5 p.m.

You will see from my photograph that my hair is no
longer dark – the blonde highlights were an attempt to
camouflage the grey! Also, I don't have blue eyes, but dark
green. These fortunately didn't change with age!

I look forward to hearing from you very soon.

Yours, always,

Angela x

I had chosen a time between 2 and 5 p.m. so that I could be sure
that I would be alone when he called. Katharine didn't return
home until 5, sometimes later, so I could be sure of having the
house to myself. But it meant that from the day after I posted the

letter, every day between 2 and 5 p.m. I'd be on pins. I didn't dare go into the garden for fear of missing his call, and became agitated every time the phone rang and it wasn't him. As the hours passed, so my nervousness grew.

If the eight weeks I'd spent with my baby son had gone too quickly, these felt like the longest four days of my life. For it was on the fourth day that he rang, at 4 p.m. precisely. It was a Friday, and my working week done, I'd been in the kitchen, wading through a big pile of ironing, when the phone went. My pulse thudded in my temple as I walked towards the telephone, picked it up and answered with my number.

'Hello,' said a male voice. 'It's James.'

Some seconds passed before I was able to compose myself sufficiently to get anything but a squeak out of my mouth. Oh my God, it was *him*. My son was on the other end of a telephone line and speaking to me! It was such a silly thing to feel awed and overwhelmed by – after all, we'd exchanged letters, hadn't we? – but that's how I felt, even so.

I don't know what I said back to him. Not my name. He knew it was me, of course he did. Was it 'hello'? Was it 'hi there'? I don't know. It's all gone. I know I was speechless for some seconds, trying to keep a lid on the fizz of my excitement. Thirty years, thirty *years* . . . I so didn't want his first impression of his birth mother to be a high-pitched hysterical babble. But, happily, he took over and began speaking again.

'I'm at work,' he said. 'So I won't be able to talk for very long, I'm afraid . . .'

'Oh yes, of *course*,' I got out.

'When are you free? So we can meet?' And then a pause, while he cleared his throat. 'I'm sorry,' he went on then. 'I really can't believe I'm so nervous.'

He would tell me later that he had felt like he'd been given the phone number of a girl and was ringing her up to ask her out for a date: not sure of her reaction, very keen to impress, tongue-tied, dry-mouthed – not at all like someone speaking to his mother.

'Me too!' I said. 'Me *too*. I've been on pins since I wrote to you! Um ... the 18th, I was thinking might be a good day, if you can do it. My daughter – no, *Kate* – *Kate's* going on a French exchange trip. To Lyon. I have to drop her at school first thing in the morning, then I'm free. I could drive to meet you, so ...'

'Um, let's have a look then ...' I could hear him flicking pages. 'That might work for me,' he said. '18th ... 18th ... Yes. I can definitely do that. So, where shall we meet?'

He had a deep voice and a London accent. I definitely remember noting the London accent.

'Maybe a hotel? Or a restaurant? I don't mind.' *I'm just desperate*, I thought, *just so desperate to see you*.

'How about a hotel, then?' he said. 'Then we won't have to worry about parking.'

I couldn't have imagined worrying about anything less.

'I can't do this,' I told Monty, as I took him out for a walk half an hour later. He didn't normally go for walks at this time – Michael liked to take him out when he got home from work at 6.30 – but I'd been too agitated and excited to stay indoors any longer, and since we'd had another cold snap lying on the hammock wasn't an option. I also knew Katharine would be home before long, and if I was going to keep up any sort of façade of normality, I needed to get out, stretch my legs and calm down.

Now I'd spoken to James, and told James about *her*, I felt even more keenly that it wasn't right to keep her in the dark about *him*. And having arranged to meet him – quite deliberately – on the day she was leaving for her trip, I felt worse. How could I drop her, in all conscience, and then drive off to meet him? I couldn't. It felt all wrong. I'd been keeping this secret from her for almost two weeks now and, however much I took Michael's arguments on board, my conscience was weighing heavily on me.

We didn't have secrets like this between us. She was my only daughter – my only child, as far as she knew – and we had always shared everything. There was nothing she couldn't confide in me about, and she knew she could rely on me to be honest with her, always. The thought of this momentous event happening behind her back – when she wasn't even in the country, moreover – felt like a betrayal of her trust.

Then I remembered Frances Holmes's comment, in her letter, about getting in touch with her if I needed advice. That was what I needed to do – I needed to call her. She might not have the definitive answer, but at least she could talk it through with me. I checked my watch then, and realised it would be too late to call now – so it would have to wait until after the weekend.

I felt a little guilty that I called Frances Holmes while Michael was at work on the Monday, but as I dialled the number and waited for the call to be answered, I think I already knew what

I should do. Even so, it would be good to hear if she considered my choice to be the right one. All that had happened – James finding me, the prospect of him becoming a part of our lives – was not, after all, just about me. And immediately Frances made me feel better.

'I'm so glad you called,' she said warmly. 'I've been thinking about you and James. How are things going?'

I told her about our phone call and our forthcoming meeting. Even relating this to her, it felt like a dream. I then outlined my uncertainty about when to tell Katharine. 'Oh, sooner rather than later, in almost all cases,' she told me. 'That's what we advise.'

'That's so good to hear,' I told her. 'I've hated keeping it from her.'

'I'm sure,' she agreed. 'It's such a big thing to happen to you all. But you know what I would advise first? That you call NORCAP as well. They're the experts. Talk it through with them. And anything else you're concerned about. They're tremendously helpful and have lots of experience. Of course it's not just about the initial revelations and how you handle them; it's also the ongoing adjustments that you'll all need to make. Do speak to them, if you can. I know you'll find it useful.'

NORCAP, it turned out, was the National Organisation for Counselling Adoptees and Parents, and as soon as I'd taken down their number and said goodbye to Frances, I called them too. They were as helpful and reassuring as she'd predicted.

'You should definitely go ahead and tell her,' the counsellor told me. 'Teenagers are remarkably resilient about these kinds of things, much more so than you probably imagine. She doesn't have the emotional investment in your son at this stage, remember, so even were things not to work out for you all, she will easily adjust. Far better that than keeping it from her, because the latter course – if she finds out – is likely to upset her so much more. There will be an adjustment for her to make, of course, once it sinks in that she's not your only child. If she has any sense that she's been excluded along the way, it will actually make that transition harder.'

I worried then about the damage I might have done already. 'Should I have told her before, when she was little?' I asked. 'I didn't because there didn't seem to be any point; not if he was never going to be a part of our lives.'

'Not at all. You did right,' she reassured me. 'What's important is how you handle this *new* situation. That you make sure she's part of the process of you all being reunited. That's what matters: how you take things from here.'

I put the phone down feeling that a great weight had been lifted from me, and resolved that, whatever Michael said, I *was* going to tell her. I was going to tell her, I decided, that very night.

Michael still didn't agree, and I had to respect that. I could understand why; after all, he wasn't swept up in my euphoric state, was he? So he was much better placed to see the potential pitfalls. But he could also see I was determined. Now I'd actually spoken to James, he was reassured and feeling more optimistic about the outcome. We agreed that, at a prearranged time after dinner, he'd call Katharine down to come and talk to me – she'd invariably be upstairs revising on weeknights – and then take Monty out while I told her.

*

It's the right of every mother to be subjective about their offspring, so I make no apology for saying that my seventeen-year-old daughter had become a beautiful young woman. She was beautiful on the outside and on the inside. She was thoughtful and caring, and always sensitive to others' emotions; she was personable, engaging and true to herself. She had been a joy to raise, a delight to us both, in every way, and barely a day went by when I didn't count my blessings that I had been lucky enough to have her. I couldn't imagine life without her, and trusted she felt the same.

I hoped, I *so* hoped, she'd understand. That was my principal emotion as I sat in the living room waiting for her, the package of letters and photos on my lap – hope that she'd understand, and forgive me.

Michael had by now got Monty's lead out and clipped it on. He poked his head round the door and gave me a smile and a thumbs-up.

'I'll give you an hour,' he said. 'Might do a quick detour to the pub . . . Kate!' he called then, up the stairs. 'Can you come down a minute? Mummy's got something important that she needs to talk to you about.'

I heard her bedroom door open, and fingered the battered manila envelope nervously. Up until now, it hadn't contained very much, my precious package, but the few tangible things I *did* have of my son, I had kept and cherished for three decades. Now it also contained James's letter, as well as the photographs he'd sent me.

'Sorry, did you call, Daddy?' I heard Katharine say to

Michael. She'd been listening to music, no doubt, and hadn't heard him clearly. He repeated his request, and then I heard her coming down. 'Mummy's in the living room,' he said to her, then he was gone.

'What's happened, Mummy?' she asked as she came in, eyeing my battered envelope warily. She was followed by a swirl of cold air. 'Are you okay?' She looked worried. No – more than that, frightened.

'I'm *fine*,' I reassured her, patting the sofa beside me. 'But I have something to tell you that is going to change your life.'

She blinked at me, her eyes filling with tears as I said this and, seeing it, I felt flustered, not really knowing where to start. In the end, I didn't try. I just reached into the envelope and pulled out Frances Holmes's letter, and then, as she read that, the dog-eared cardboard cot tag that I had untied the day my baby and I had both left Loreto Convent. '*Paul Brown*,' it said on it. '*Weight at birth: 8 lbs 12 oz*.'

I handed the card to her as she lowered the letter. I had toyed with trying to explain Frances's carefully coded message, but my daughter was a bright girl; with the card in her hand, she'd soon work it out. I was right. When she looked up at me, I could see comprehension dawning.

At last I could tell her my story.

Chapter Twenty-One

Katharine's initial reaction was one of relief. And the reason for those tears was now obvious. Why had I been so naive? Of *course* she'd have known something was up. And how stupid had I been not to realise her first thought would be that I was keeping something terrible from her?

'I thought you were ill,' she confessed, through huge, racking sobs. We were both crying freely now, albeit for different reasons. 'I really thought you were going to tell me something devastating. You looked so *serious*. And all Daddy's pointed remarks about taking Monty for a long walk. I thought you had *cancer*, Mummy—'

Oh, God, I thought. My poor, poor daughter. 'Oh, Kate. I'm so sorry . . .'

'I thought those' – she poked a finger towards the offending brown envelope – 'were *X-rays*, some horrible X-rays you were about to pull out. Honestly, Mummy, I've been *so* worried about you! You've been so strange. So not *you*.'

I hung my head, chastened. 'I know. And I'm so, so sorry. I didn't mean to be. I didn't *want* to be. And I'm sorry I didn't tell you when the letter came from Mrs Holmes. I just didn't want to tell you till he got in touch with me himself. Until I knew for sure – till both Daddy and I did – that it was all really going to happen, that I hadn't dreamt it.'

She threw her arms around my neck then, scattering the little pile of treasures on my lap. 'Oh, but Mummy, I can't believe it. I have a brother! Photos . . . you said you had photos, a photo of him now . . . yes? I'm dying to see what he looks like!'

I leaned down, scooped up the photos and handed her the one of James. He was standing alone, somewhere foreign – the Mediterranean, perhaps, was my guess. He looked tanned, and was in shorts.

She stared at it without speaking for some moments. How weird it must be, I thought, to think yourself an only child and then to be presented with a picture of a brother you didn't know existed. I hoped it would be weird in a good way. I certainly knew she couldn't fail to see the likeness. 'Oh. My. *God*,' she said slowly. 'He looks just like you, Mummy! And me! Look . . . the same eyes, the same hair, the same skin . . .' She grinned at me, her expression incredulous.

'And Uncle Ray, I thought. Don't you think he looks so much like Uncle Ray?'

'God, *yes*! Yes he does! Amazing . . .' She shook her head. 'This is my big *brother*! I can't believe how lucky I am – I really can't!'

But this wasn't just something to get excited about. It was also, for my sensitive teenage daughter, something beyond reason or comprehension. Once she'd absorbed the reality of having this new big brother, and had asked me all about him, her thoughts returned to the circumstances of his birth and adoption, both of which perplexed her. Why on earth was I made to give him up? How could society have been so backward? How could girls be treated so appallingly in the name of religion? Why could I *not* have been taken care of? Why couldn't a solution have been found? She quizzed me at length about this, her expression thoughtful. And, as I tried to answer her questions, she became increasingly angry on my behalf.

'I mean it's just so *wrong*,' she said. 'How could they *do* that and have any sort of conscience?'

'Society was just different then,' I tried to explain. 'An unmarried mother was a pariah.'

'But to *whom*, exactly? How could people call themselves Christians and then treat other human beings in such an unchristian way?'

That was difficult to answer, because I'd asked myself that same question many times. I said so. 'But it wasn't just Christians,' I went on. 'Many people in those days felt the same – the majority, I'd say. If you got pregnant and weren't married, you really were shunned, not just by the Catholic Church but by "polite" society. You were the lowest of the low.'

'Whereas the fathers – the men who made women pregnant in the first place – I bet they got away with it scot-free.'

'Very often,' I agreed. 'Yes, of course they did. It wasn't seen as their problem. And often, in reality, it wasn't. It was the woman's responsibility because it was the woman who had the baby.'

'And not that much has changed,' she said thoughtfully. 'But it's still so incredible that you could be sent away like that, and made to feel so shameful. And forced to have your baby away from everyone, all on your own, with no one to care for you. And then to have to hand the baby over. I mean, how could anyone have thought that was okay?'

'I don't think anyone really thought it was "okay",' I said. 'I think people just thought there was no other solution.'

'But not *everyone*, surely? Some girls *must* have kept their babies.'

'I'm sure they did. If they had the support at home, I suppose they must have. Sometimes a girl's parents would bring up the child with them, and pretend the mother was an older sister – that sort of thing. But for others—'

'Like your mother . . .' Her expression was pointed now.

'Well, it wasn't an option, no, not in a million years. Not financially; not socially. The Church, religion, faith . . . well, it's complicated, isn't it? Religion's a powerful force in the world.'

'I don't think it's that complicated,' Katharine argued. 'Not at all. Not when it's your child you're talking about, surely? I mean, how could your own mother have put you *through* that? It's barbaric. I mean how can you say someone's a bad person because they accidentally get pregnant? And then treat them so badly – take their *own child* away from them – and then claim the moral high ground? That seems much more immoral to me!'

I understood her reasoning. She lived in such a vastly changed world. 'It was a different time,' I said again. 'It's hard to accept now, I know, but that was just the way things were. People *did* accept it. *I* accepted it. We all did. I got myself into trouble and

I had to take the consequences. Gran was only doing what she thought was the right thing.'

'But still,' she persisted. 'Someone should have been looking after you! I mean, can you imagine?' She picked up the photo of James as a baby, and the cot tag. 'I mean, think about it,' she said. 'You were hardly any older than I am now, were you? And you had to go to that horrible place, all on your own, and live with a bunch of strangers, and then go and have your baby, all on your own *again*, only to have them take it away from you! I mean, think about it, Mummy. Can you imagine putting *me* through that? *Can* you?'

My daughter's words did make me think. Could I ever imagine that? No, of course not. I'd have rather put myself through it – and more – than see my child suffer the way I had. But I also knew that forgiving my mother had been one of the most important things I'd ever done.

She had died of a heart attack in 1985, just two years after Sam had died. One of the things I'd reflected on after receiving James's letter was that she hadn't lived to know that I had been reunited with the child she had made me give up.

We'd never spoken of it again, not in detail, not in passing, not even obliquely. Though I understood this was the only way she could deal with what had happened, it still upset me, particularly in the early years, to have my own hurt unacknowledged. I didn't expect her to apologise – as I'd said to Katharine, my mother had only done what she'd thought was right – but it would have been a comfort to know that she did at least acknowledge my distress.

If I'd learned anything in my life as a result of my upbringing and my religion, it was forgiveness. And when God had forgiven me – which, in giving me my precious daughter, I believed He had done – then it seemed only right that I should feel able to forgive my mother. I did it for myself as well: it wouldn't have been healthy to spend the rest of my life feeling bitter. It would have been like a canker, eating away at my soul.

Instead I have been blessed in so many ways in my life. I had found Michael, I had my beautiful daughter, I wanted for nothing and I made a point of counting those blessings, often. Had God seen that, I wondered, and stepped in to repay my stoicism by allowing me to get to know my son at last? A bit of a fanciful notion, probably nonsense, but it seemed apposite, even so.

Despite the excitement, despite the joy, despite my son's evident pleasure in having tracked me down, one big question – perhaps *the* big question – still remained: would James be able to forgive me?

Katharine wrote to me that evening, the sweetest, loveliest letter, in an attempt to order the thoughts she'd not yet been able to when we spoke. She told me how thrilled she was for me, and how much she understood my reticence about telling her before. And she wanted to let me know again just how thrilled she was for herself, because now she might finally have that older brother she'd been hankering after all her life.

'Oh, but I'm so upset I'm going to be missing out on all of this!' she said, as we clambered out of the car, ready to meet the school coach. It was 18 February and we had arrived at her school in Sevenoaks, ready for her and the other girls to make the trip to Gatwick Airport, from where they'd fly to Lyon for their ten-day stay.

She pulled the boot open and yanked out her holdall. 'I don't want to go now, I really don't. I don't even like her!'

The 'her' in question was Isabella. She was the French girl Katharine had been paired with and who'd come to stay with us the previous October. And I did sympathise. Though we'd tried hard to make her welcome, she didn't seem to want to be here. She was rather sullen and a bit petulant. I felt for my daughter. They had little in common. I felt a pang of guilt that she not only had to miss out on the 'big event' with James, but she also had to go and stay at the home of a girl when she'd really rather not.

'You'll have a great time,' I told her, reassuringly. 'I know you will. It's not like it's just you on your own, after all. You'll be doing loads of group activities, and Lyon is lovely, a fabulous city. Just think of her house as somewhere to sleep. After all, that's all it is, really . . .'

'But I want to see James! Oh, I'm so jealous. The biggest and most exciting thing to have happened in my *whole LIFE,* and I'm not even going to be involved!'

We walked across to where a small gaggle of girls and parents were assembling. As we did so, she slipped her arm through mine. I knew she wasn't angry with me; she was just sad and a bit down. Not only did she not really want to go to France in the first place, she now had the best possible reason not to go. But it was part of her A-level course. And it was only ten days, I kept telling myself. She would enjoy it when she got there, I felt sure.

Given Katharine's excitement at meeting her new brother, I had wondered about seeing if I could meet him sooner, so that perhaps she could meet him too before she left. But I'd opted not to do that, having decided, with Michael's agreement, that the first meeting needed to be alone – just the two of us. Even had I tried to make it sooner, that would have left little time to cram in another meeting to introduce James and Katharine to each other. We needed to take things one step – one giant step – at a time.

'I'll be right by the phone from the minute I get home,' I told her. 'So you can ring me the very minute you arrive and I'll be able to sit down and tell you all about him. Okay?'

She sighed resignedly. 'I suppose it'll have to be,' she sniffed, 'won't it?' She looked past me. 'Ah, there's Clare!' She waved at her friend. 'I guess we'd better get going if we're going to get a decent seat.' She threw her arms around me.

'Safe journey,' I said. 'And have a really good trip.'

'And you have one too, and a brilliant time with James.' She stood back then and appraised me. 'You look lovely, Mummy. Perfect. Oh, he's going to love you *so* much!'

Chapter Twenty-Two

James and I had agreed to meet up in a hotel in Brentwood, in Essex, because it was halfway between his home in Cambridgeshire and mine in Kent.

It's a Holiday Inn nowadays, an anonymous-looking, fifties-style, low-rise hotel of the kind you tend to find huddled in groups just off motorways. Then, as now, it was the perfect bolthole for businessmen and an anonymous location for clandestine couples. Back then it was, I think, a Trusthouse Forte, but little different from how it is today.

I'd driven up from Sevenoaks in a Jekyll-and-Hyde frame of mind, my impatience to get there and see my son tempered by waves of anxiety, as all the 'what ifs' of the situation, now irreversibly drilled into me by Michael, reminded me that I was off to meet a stranger. Genes and those scant early weeks we'd spent together aside, that was what he was – a man I didn't know.

Getting ready that morning, I'd been as nervous as any teenager getting ready for a date. I wasn't playing a part – I could only be what I was, after all – but I was also desperate to impress. How could I not be?

In his mind, as he was growing up, I was the mother who'd given birth to him and then abandoned him. So one of the first things I had to do was set the record straight, and convince him just how much I had loved and yearned for him since. I was also conscious that he must have spent many of those intervening thirty years imagining me, forming a picture in his head, just as I had done of him, without anything to go on but his mirror. How much time had he spent wondering who I was, where I was, how I'd fared and what had become of me?

I thought about his comment that his mother was an 'Essex Girl', so I took great trouble not to dress like one, even though I wasn't completely sure what I'd have worn if I had been one.

Katharine had found the whole thing hilarious. 'Mummy, stop worrying!' she'd told me, over and over. 'He will so blatantly *love* you!'

I remembered the words in her letter to me: '*I feel confident, as I hope you do, that he will want to remain in touch with us for the rest of our lives, and just remember if, by any remote, slight, far-off chance, Paul doesn't want to continue what he's started, then it's his loss, because he is missing out on knowing the best mother anyone could have.*' Her words were so sweet, so touching and such a comfort to me.

I kept them in mind now, as I sped round the M25. It was almost 10.00 now, the tail end of the Friday morning rush hour, and I couldn't get there fast enough. I'd dressed demurely but normally in the end, in clothes that I knew I'd feel relaxed wearing: a crisp white blouse, a navy and green woollen pencil skirt, a navy blazer with brass buttons and penny loafers. I probably looked like a middle-aged woman attending an interview, which, in a way, was precisely what I was doing, wasn't I? Can I be in your life now? Can I have a role to play? A purpose? Please just like me . . . oh, please learn to *love* me.

The journey seemed interminable. But it wasn't quite long enough, paradoxically, because as I pulled off the motorway and approached the hotel car park, I felt as if I were about to sit an important exam but had left all my crib notes at home, that I was winging it, completely unprepared.

What must it be like for him? I wondered as I climbed out of my car. I glanced across at the mass of other vehicles. The hotel must be busy – the car park was almost full. Which one of these might be his, I thought? The big in-your-face BMW? The rugged four by four? The sensible Volvo? Which one? What sort of car might appeal to him?

I locked my own car. Was he even here yet, come to that? Was he an early sort of person or a late sort of person? There were so many little details to be discovered about him. Since he was a policeman, I decided he was probably the former, and I would turn out to be quite wrong.

I checked the time – it was around 10.50. There was no one around and no point in waiting out in the cold. I swung my bag up to my shoulder and strode into the hotel.

The hotel clearly was having some refurbishment work done. There was a ceiling-high dust sheet billowing in the draught created by my entrance, screening off what I imagined was the lounge and bar.

I stood in the lobby, scanning the remaining area for anyone who might be him. I could see no one. Stupidly self-conscious and twitchy with nerves, I went across to a stand full of leaflets for tourists, and began plucking them randomly from their slots. There were lots of them – so much to do in and around Brentwood! – but they were lost on me. I don't think I read a line. Every few seconds I would glance out of the corner of my eye, trying to spot the face that looked like the one in the photograph.

And then, suddenly, there he was, appearing before me as if by magic, having come from behind the plastic sheeting. There was no way I could ever have mistaken his identity. He was so much my darling son, it made the hairs on the back of my neck prickle. I savoured every moment of those magical first seconds between seeing him and the instant that our eyes met.

It was one of the most incredible things I can recall feeling ever in my life. It was like seeing myself first – bizarrely – and then my lost baby, repackaged in the form of this stranger. He was so tall, dark and handsome that it left me open-mouthed.

My dear, *dear* son. I'd imagined so many versions of this encounter over the years, spooled so many movie trailer moments in my head of how I'd be and how he might be and all the things we'd say to each other. But when it came to it, no words were necessary. There was no time for uncomfortable air-kisses or stilted handshaking, and thoughts of exchanging formal words of greeting got swept away. We just met in the middle and fell into one another's arms. As I hugged him, all I could think of was that terrible day at the Crusade of Rescue, and the kiss I hadn't been able to place on his cheek. To be able to kiss him now felt like a miracle.

I don't know what anyone must have thought had they seen us – a smart middle-aged woman embracing a good-looking young man. But, actually, would they have thought anything? That we were mother and son was so gloriously evident.

When we separated, both of us were crying.

'I wasn't going to do that,' James said gruffly. 'I had promised myself I wasn't going to do that.'

I was already rummaging in my handbag for tissues for us both. 'I'm so glad you did,' I replied.

How do you cover thirty years in an afternoon? It's impossible, but we did our very best to.

'It was in Turkey,' James explained, after we'd revisited almost everything in our letters to each other, and more, 'where that photo I sent you was taken. That was when I finally made my mind up. I'd spent so long wanting to, really wanting to, and then – well, just failing to find the courage, I guess. I was just too terrified of being told to go away.'

'Oh, how I wish,' I said, 'how I so wish you could have known how much I longed for that to happen. I can't tell you how much.'

'Well, you have Karen to thank,' he said. 'She was the one who made it happen. Because that was what *she* said, pretty much. How did I know I'd be rejected? Why was I so sure you'd turn me away? And she was right. I'd never really thought of it that way – you know, seen it from that standpoint. For all I thought about you, I suppose it had never occurred to me to see it from a mother's point of view.' He smiled. 'Perhaps it needed a woman's imagination. The way Karen put it to me, it seemed so much less terrifying. She said that if she put herself in your shoes – you know, given the time we were in then, the social mores, the conventions – she couldn't imagine having to give a child up and *not* spending every day after that wondering about them, worrying about them, hoping for a chance to find them again one day.'

'Three cheers for Karen, then,' I said. 'No, make it four!'

'So I did it right away,' he went on, 'before I could chicken out again. Almost the day after we got back I think it must have been, I got on to the Crusade of Rescue. And then I went there and saw your file, and it was just so incredibly emotional. You know, finding out what they knew about you, that you had two brothers and so on. And that was emotional in itself, knowing I had these two uncles and wondering if they even knew of my existence. Weird. And I'm so sorry your mother's gone. I would have liked to meet my grandmother.'

'I would, too,' I said, 'I really would have loved her to meet you. I think knowing we'd found each other would have been so precious to her. I'm sure it would have gone a long way towards assuaging her guilt.'

He picked up his coffee and drained the cup – we must have been on our fourth now. Plus we'd had prawn sandwiches – what a joy that we both liked prawn sandwiches. We continued to make all sorts of joyful discoveries about each other and how alike we were in so many little ways.

'But listen,' he said now, his expression serious, 'I really must make it clear to you that I don't want to disrupt your life. Not for a minute. Not if this, well, you know, isn't what you want. I mean, for me, this is the best thing imaginable – meeting you, getting to know you – but I don't want you to feel pressured or for this to cause problems within your family. I would hate that. It wouldn't be fair.'

I could imagine him speaking to Frances Holmes about this. My heart went out to him for saying what must have been such a difficult thing to contemplate: that, having found me, I might want to put him back in a box marked 'the past'. 'James, believe me,' I said, once again having to reach for tissues. 'That couldn't be further from the truth. I have *longed* for this day. I don't think I'll ever be able to express to you quite how much. Just ask Michael – my husband. He's known about you all along. And he's been *such* a support to me. As have my whole family – both those brothers, especially, and my lovely sisters-in-law. You might not have been with us physically, but you've always still been *with* us, you know, in our hearts. And as for Kate—'

'*Is* she okay with this? I mean, *really* okay? I can't wait to meet *her*, but is she really all right? Surely she must feel some resentment about me coming into your life? It must be difficult for her, especially if she's been brought up an only child, surely?'

I shook my head. 'She couldn't be more excited about meeting you. She can't wait.' I told him about having to wave her off before coming to meet him, and how much she had wished she could be with us instead. 'Honestly,' I said, 'she thinks you're the best thing that's ever happened to her – and I mean that. Those were her exact words.'

He frowned. 'Oh, dear, I have a lot to live up to, then. I hope I don't prove to be a massive disappointment!'

We talked for hours, until the lunch crowd had been replaced by the afternoon stragglers, and by the time we started to think about leaving, the early evening gaggles of men in suits, carrying briefcases, were beginning to congregate too. We were oblivious to them all, our attention wholly on each other.

It was dark when we emerged and walked back to the car park. His car, it turned out, had been a nondescript Vauxhall. 'Police car,' he clarified, with a wink, 'an unmarked one. But hang on,' he said then, as we reached my car, which was nearer. 'I've got something for you. I'll be back in just a tick.'

I watched as he loped off to his car in the darkness, thrilling again at our physical similarities. My son. This was my *son*. I couldn't stop marvelling at the fact. And as I watched him go, I was already imagining telling Michael and Katharine – especially Katharine, whom I now needed to get home for. It was getting late, and I couldn't miss her call. I really mustn't, and in France, of course, she'd already be an hour ahead of me. *He's gorgeous*, I would tell her. *He's lovely, he's funny, he's clever. He looks like you do! He'll be a brilliant big brother. You will love him.*

He returned carrying something, and as he got closer I could see it was a bouquet of flowers – lilies and gerberas and beautifully fragrant roses. He handed them to me, looking both pleased as punch and bashful all at once. I loved that. I loved *him*. It felt as natural as breathing. I took the flowers. There was a card tucked within them, which I could see he had written himself. It read *'I'm very, very happy for both of us. Yours always, James xxxx'*

For the umpteenth time that day, I was speechless and in tears. How many tears of joy had I shed today, I wondered? And how many more had been shed in wretchedness and sorrow over the years? So many – too many. And as I hugged him once again, I think he must have known what I was thinking, for he put his lips close to my ear and spoke for both of us.

'Drive safely,' he whispered, as he kissed me farewell. 'Now I've found you, I don't want to lose you.'

Epilogue

I n fairy stories, the traditional way to finish is to reassure the reader that all concerned lived happily ever after. And to date, I'm pleased to say, that has mostly been true for us, though our story has not been without further bouts of heartache.

Finding someone like Michael to share my life with, having my miracle-baby daughter, being blessed with my gorgeous grandchildren – Katharine's three little ones and James's two. These are the things that really matter in life. Being reunited with my son, after three decades of longing, was also one of the happiest times imaginable.

James and I established a relationship, and a friendship, very quickly. Within days of my meeting him, he brought his fiancée Karen down to stay with us, and Katharine was finally able to meet the brother she'd always wanted. It was, for all of us, a very happy time. To see such likenesses, to introduce him to his other extended family and to have him count us as part of his were such enriching and rewarding experiences. Beyond rewarding is how I recall thinking of it at the time.

We were also invited to James and Karen's wedding. And it was then, perhaps, that I first had to confront the reality of the life

James had led that hadn't included me. Where those thirty years, in my case, had always been tinged with the continuing pain of his absence, he had felt no such lack; at least not until he'd grown into a teenager and had begun to explore his feelings about where he'd come from and why.

He'd had a mother and father, a younger sister and a whole coterie of relatives and friends. The only difference between him and any other child of his acquaintance was that there was this 'other mother' out there, who had always been a mystery.

Looking back now, I wonder how his adoptive mother must have felt when she heard we had been invited to James's wedding. It's an intense enough time emotionally, seeing your child get married, so for her to have to accommodate as big a thing as James wanting to invite us along too must have been difficult, to say the least.

To help minimise any possible awkwardness on the day, we had already met James's parents. He had arranged for Michael and me to go to Cambridgeshire to visit them. By now they were both retired schoolteachers – they'd been quite a bit older than me, obviously – and they couldn't have been more kind and welcoming. Though James's father, Michael, had dark hair, his parents bore no physical similarity to him. I wonder how difficult it must have been for them both to see how much James looked like me. Perhaps not at all – they had, after all, entered into the adoption process, just as we had as potential parents, with a clear idea of what might lie ahead. Even so, I could readily put myself in their shoes. This was a turning point in their lives every bit as much as in ours. For me, certainly, it was strange to put faces to the voices that I'd heard all that time ago at the Crusade of Rescue, when I was almost stupefied by pain and mental anguish.

They'd seen me, they told me, as I'd walked out of the building that afternoon. They'd been in that room, Paul now asleep in his new mother's arms, when they saw me, lugging my holdall, trudging down the darkening street. They had wondered, as James's father commented to me when we met him, how I must have been feeling that day.

But, just as I did, they'd left and got on with their lives, and cherished the son they'd felt so lucky to have been blessed with. Though him wanting to seek me out some day wasn't inevitable, they'd never shied away from reminding him where he'd come from, and had made it clear that if he did want to find his birth mother, they would never stand in his way. James's journey to find me, even so, had been a long one. Once he'd made the decision – on the day he'd set the date for his wedding to Karen – the first thing he'd done was tell his parents. As he'd put in his letter, they had never tried to dissuade him, but it had taken a great deal of soul-searching for him to pluck up the courage.

His fear of rejection by me a second time was too great – and he had reason to suspect that might happen. In 1976, there was a significant change in adoption law. To make it easier for adopted children to trace their birth parents, they now had the legal right of access to their adoption records. But this was not the only change.

Unbeknown to me, there was another important amendment to the law at around that time. It involved the creation of a new

Adoption Register, in which the birth parents of adopted children, previously only traceable with difficulty, could have their names and current contact details put on file. Once he had decided he felt strong enough to accept whatever he uncovered, it was naturally to this document that James first turned. Not finding my name on it – as he wouldn't, since I didn't even know of its existence – he could only conclude that his reservations were well founded. To his mind, this was evidence that I was one of the overwhelming majority of birth parents who actively didn't want to be found.

Having got that far, however, he had a change of heart. The closer he got to finding me, it seemed, the more he wavered about doing so, as all the negative scenarios dominated his thoughts. Having all but decided to abandon his search, for fear of what he might find, he was persuaded by Karen to carry on. Knowing him as well as she unquestionably did, she knew how troubled he'd always been about not knowing where he came from and how desperately he needed that missing piece of the jigsaw in place. So, supported by her, he continued his search, finally realising himself that even if he did get rejected in the end, it was still better than living with the mystery.

By now he had enough information to pursue things on his own. He had a name – Angela Brown – and my parents' address in Rayleigh. He knew that I'd been a codes translator, and I had two elder brothers.

It was here that his job as a policemen was to give James a great advantage over many people seeking lost relatives. One other piece of information he had about me was my national insurance number, as it formed a part of my original records. As a person's NI number stays with them for life, it's a good tool, if known, with which to track them down. James was lucky, then; most people don't have legal access to such information. The world is full of stories of adopted children spending years trying to find their birth parents, only to be too late and find that by the time they've been found, they've passed on.

To James's excitement, however, and my subsequent delight, his position meant he could access an up-to-date address for me straight away. Such was his gratitude at having the tools to do this that he would eventually go on to help Frances Holmes at the Catholic Children's Society with a number of terribly sad and very urgent cases.

When James saw an Angela Patrick and Michael Patrick at the address given on the database, his immediate assumption – which was reasonable, based on the scant information he had to go on – was that I was a single mother with another, now adult, child. He was finally decided. What would be, would be. He got back in touch with Frances.

James could obviously have pursued me himself. There was nothing to stop him from simply writing to me directly, but Frances, with whom he'd initially made contact, had strenuously counselled against it. As an adoption agency, one of the saddest parts of what they did was to help steer a course through the emotional journey adopted children took when they decided to try and find their birth parents.

As James had told me when we'd got in touch, he was one of the few lucky ones, as almost all of the birth parents who responded (few in themselves) only confirmed what was statistically proven: that they didn't want to be reunited with the children they'd given up. It was important to the society that they were there for the adoptees, both to be realistic about outcomes and to be there for them in the event of bad news.

This was why the letter I'd received, so cleverly worded, so cleverly coded, came from Frances, rather than James himself. It was also part of their policy to encourage further correspondence before meetings, to give both adoptee and birth parent a time to think things through – allowing for a 'cooling-off' period – before further life-changing decisions were made.

Both of us agreed, later, that we had been champing at the bit. But Frances had been right: it was only sensible to proceed slowly.

But James and I finding one another was, as it turned out, only the beginning of a new story, one that began around the time, in the summer of 1995, when his marriage to Karen sadly broke up. He'd met someone else and was by this time also travelling a great deal with his job. He had done well in the police force, moving up steadily through the ranks, and by now was working undercover much of the time, and out of anyone's reach for days at a stretch. Understandably, given both his career and his ever-changing locations, it was difficult to find times to get together. We'd often plan trips and visits and, increasingly often, he'd phone to cancel at the last minute.

I tried hard to be reasonable and philosophical about all this. I would tell myself constantly that having him in my life *at all* was such a gift. It was something I'd hoped for so much but had never expected, something I had so longed for but knew I had no right to. But no matter how hard or how often I tried to rein in my feelings, they would bubble up unbidden and take me over.

It came to a head one day, in 1996, during a phone call in which he explained that he had to pull out of a trip to Ireland, which, though nothing major – it was just a couple of days to visit relatives on my mother's side – had been planned with his agreement. I had just needed to confirm the flight times, which was why I'd called him.

'I'm sorry,' he'd told me. 'But I can't make it, after all. I know I should have called sooner, but you know how it is.'

I was devastated to hear this, perhaps wrongly, perhaps irrationally. Did it matter *that* much? It was only a few days away. But on top of so many other instances of feeling let down and superfluous to him, my emotions got the better of my usual clear-headedness. I'd been longing to show him off to all these members of my family, and I couldn't seem to get past feeling hurt.

'Yes, perhaps you should,' I'd answered, irritably. 'All this time I've been waiting to hear, and only *now* do I find out—'

'Look, I'm sorry,' he interrupted, his tone equally irritable. 'But I do have another family to think about here. I have commitments. I have a sister. I have other people to see. I have other things in my life apart from you.'

It was all true, and I didn't need to be told any of it, really. Even so, I felt summarily dismissed when he said that, as if I were just a minor part of his life, and should know my place.

'I know that,' I remember saying to him, full of pique. 'I *do*. I'm just unhappy at the way you treat *me*!'

And then, those fateful words having finally spilled out, I was too upset to go on. I put the phone down.

It probably had to happen, that phone call that day. Though his words haunted me, and the sense of rejection was so painful, it probably had to happen that I articulated the feelings that had been simmering away in me since the day we had found each other. Perhaps it needed to happen to help me see beyond myself; to think about our unusual situation logically and objectively, to admit to the jealous longing I harboured. Hard though it was, I perhaps needed to realise that though I was his birth mother, I wasn't his mother. And I had no right to expect him to treat me as such.

Having thought all this through – and it took me some days and weeks to do so – I decided I wouldn't make further contact with him. It was so hard, but I felt it was the only thing to do. He knew where I was, he knew how I felt – he knew, without doubt now, just how much I loved him – and if he wanted me in his life again, it must be his choice, not mine. It was not my place to pressure him to see me.

Weeks passed and turned into months, and still no word came from James. When my birthday came and went with no acknowledgement from him I was wretched.

'This is ridiculous,' Michael said. 'You *must* make contact. *You* must. It doesn't matter how much you feel it ought to be him that does it, who's suffering here? *You* are. And I'd bet anything that he is as well. Don't forget, this situation is not of his making. And remember, he's had a lifetime of feeling rejected by you. And he has a *point*, sweetheart. Surely you must see that? It must be hard for him, don't forget, having to deal with two families – two *mothers*. So perhaps now is the time to be one to him. Swallow your pride. Risk him rejecting you. Just like he did. Trust me, it will be your loss if you don't.'

Michael was right, of course. He always is. But I knew I couldn't phone James. Couldn't bring myself to, because I felt much too emotional. So instead, I sat and wrote him a poem.

And I sent a copy to Katharine, too. She was studying in China by now, and I missed her dreadfully. I was also painfully aware how much all this had impacted on her too. Things not working out between James and me was very difficult for her; having been introduced to and embraced the big brother she'd always dreamed of having, she now had to accept that he was gone again. So, unbeknown to me, she decided to take action. Having read my poem, she decided to call James herself, and said much the same thing to him as Michael had to me. *Stop* this. *Mend* this. Don't be silly.

And James, to my eternal joy, phoned me.

Adoption, in many circumstances, is right for all involved. But in other cases, such as mine, and many others like mine at that time, it's the catastrophic beginning of a long, painful journey, the destination of which is unknown. So how can anyone know how to deal with it? How *do* you make up for all the years you both lost? How do you come to terms with the heartache? How do you deal with the frustrations of the past and find a way, together, to move on from it? There is only one way: truthfully and slowly.

This time, when we talked, we talked more honestly, I think. James had read my poem over and over, he told me, and had focused on one line particularly. I had written about how I should be content and give thanks for him, not waste time dwelling on what might have been and dreaming of a different outcome. And, given the circumstances of his adoption and his childhood, I must accept that his love was conditional.

But he surprised me. '*No*,' he said to me that day. 'That's not true. I just needed you to understand my situation, that's all; how hard it's been and how complicated it is now. Finding you,' he told me, 'was the best thing that ever happened to me. That blood tie's unbreakable. I think about you. I love you. And that love part, I promise, is *un*conditional.'

If ever there was an expression of forgiveness, it was that. So we began again to feel our way together, treading carefully and inching forward slowly.

We are still feeling our way. In truth, perhaps we always will be. But James was right. Whatever happens, our blood tie can never be broken.

To My Son

It was an ordinary envelope dropped on the mat
Along with various others.
An ordinary envelope, a change from a bill,
I read it through twice as my heart stood still.
This may be the chance that the son I had lost,
The son I surrendered at such a great cost,
Was searching for me.

An ordinary envelope dropped on the mat
Along with various others
But this one was different from all of the rest
For here were results of my son and his quest.
A son who is happy, healthy and mine
So precious to me despite passing of time
And now will I see?

An ordinary envelope dropped on the mat
Along with various others

Evoked such painful memories which can sometimes be
    untrue,
Yet I still see it all so clearly, that short time I had with
    you.
Those tiny hands and fingernails, my sadness at your
    tears,
Frozen in time, we two, for over thirty years.
Waiting still to see.

The ordinary envelope dropped on the mat
Along with various others,
Made the bitter tears I shed turn to tears of joy.
Tears of simple gratitude for now that this boy
Whose memory had forever invaded my day,
Was now finally going to be on his way
To see me.

An ordinary envelope dropped on the mat
Along with various others
Brought forth a meeting of body, heart and mind,
Answering questions; what would we find?
The past revealed and time's dark shadow lightened,
Our hearts united and the bond of love heightened.
My thoughts are free.

An ordinary envelope dropped on the mat
Along with various others,
Had us both rejoicing with discovery of each other.

Chilling similarities of two people, son and mother.
Questions answered, searching over, a time to build
      began;
A whole new world lay before us, to hold on to if we can.
You and me.

That ordinary envelope dropped on the mat
Along with various others,
Did not give a warning of vast voids there were to fill;
Of perilously moving fast or simply standing still.
Then chinks of disenchantment began to filter through
And this very special union was no longer strong and true.
The unspoken human frailties quickly rose above the
      surface
And this tenuous relationship had somehow lost its
      purpose.
Not to be.

No ordinary envelope dropped on the mat
Along with various others.
An unacknowledged birthday was proof that dreams I'd
      shared,
Of always being in your life and knowing that you cared,
Would never now materialise and make my life complete.
Instead just painful memories and regrets so bittersweet.
I know the pain that is in me now will never go away,
It's unrelenting, worsening, with every wasted day.
Will it ever be?

Since that ordinary envelope dropped on the mat
Along with various others,
I know I must learn to give thanks for you and not for
what might have been.
To accept that your love is conditional and to let my
feelings go unseen.
Now, as I reflect on past mistakes that led to only
sadness,
I hope for a new beginning and the return of former
gladness.
Perhaps with time and understanding we could have a
bright tomorrow
So that memories that I have of you will not always
mirror sorrow.
If it can be.

That ordinary envelope dropped on the mat
Along with various others,
Answered my prayers after thirty years, my hopes were
then fulfilled.
At last not just a memory after all that time instilled.
But the years they pass so quickly and hopes so wildly
grow,
Hope must spring eternal, though now halted in its flow.
For where once there was hope now only sadness fills my
soul.
Where dreams and plans are made now lies a gaping hole.
What is to be.

This ordinary envelope dropped on the mat
Along with various others,
Attempts to show that I am vulnerable as I tiptoe in the
       past,
Where shards of forgotten memories are shrapnel to my
       heart.
So whenever I tread clumsily don't assume it's just my
       way,
For you have the power to shatter and cast my fragments
       away.
These words are so inadequate and do not fully now
       convey
The profundity of feeling in the things I cannot say.

Acknowledgements

First and foremost, a massive thank you to my daughter Katharine, whose idea this book was, and for her encouragement and enthusiasm.

Grateful thanks to Ben Mason for having faith in my story and for his valued guidance.

Thank you to Lynne Barrett-Lee for converting my ramblings into the written word.

Thank you to Kerri Sharp and her colleagues at Simon & Schuster for all their help and advice.

Last but by no means least, huge thanks to my husband Michael for his constant and unqualified support.